Not Mentioning Any Names

Margaret Pearce

Not Mentioning
Any Names

Not Mentioning Any Names
ISBN 978 1 76109 037 0
Copyright © text Margaret Pearce 2020
Internal illustrations: Leonie McDonald
Cover: Zac Barry

First published 2020 by
GINNINDERRA PRESS
PO Box 3461 Port Adelaide 5015
www.ginninderrapress.com.au

Contents

The Lost Club	7
First Words	11
The Collecting Instinct	12
The Tomato Sauce Trick	15
Heroes Never Kiss Girls	16
Five Minutes in the Life of…	18
On Bathing Small Boys	21
The Worthy Cause	23
Pocket Money	26
The Tooth Fairy	28
The Class Raffle	30
Home Nursing	32
The Problem With Crackers	36
A Money Problem	38
A Business Enterprise	39
School lunches	41
After-school Games	44
The School Dance	46
The New Pet	49
The Cooking Disaster	51
Relationships	54
The Delicate Problem	56
The Casualty	59
The Intelligent Solution	62
How To Diet	64
The Jeans Problem	66

Hope is Not a Method	68
Homework For Parents	70
The Guinea Pig Business	72
School Sick Days	75
What to Wear	77
Clean Socks For School	80
Mother's Day	82
Low Finance	85
The Viking Funeral	87
The Lost Football	89
Lost and Found	91
Harmony	94
The Good Samaritan	95
Life in the Seventies	97
Gifts for the Grateful	99
Transport	101
High Finance	102
Rolls Royce Driving	105
Car Matters	106
Yoda	107
The Musical Talent	111
Reading to Children	113
The Guinea Pig Saga	115
Sherry	117
Having a Family	121
Acknowledgements	123

The Lost Club

My family are foundation members of the Professional Mislayers' Club.

It started when I mislaid my first baby. I left him outside a shoe store and was actually on the train home before I realised I was lacking a pram. Fortunately, lurking baby-snatchers must have overlooked him, because he was still there when I rushed back.

When he was old enough, he carried on the tradition by mislaying himself. Houdini couldn't have been more adept at opening locked doors or escaping over high barred fences.

Even Her Majesty's prisons would have had trouble confining him, and once freed, he vanished into the wider world. He clambered on buses and trams, crawled up drains or under houses, or rode his trike to shopping centres or parks.

My social life improved considerably. A steady stream of policemen, clergymen, bus drivers, shopkeepers and neighbours were always on my doorstep.

When he was old enough to be allowed the run of the streets, he kept mislaying his baby sister. He liked his baby sister and always played with her. He stuffed her like an amiable sack of potatoes into his cart and as soon as I looked away, took off.

'But where did you leave her?' I implored when I realised she and the cart were missing.

'I dunno. I got hungry and came home for my dinner,' in an aggrieved tone. 'You always tell me to come home at dinner time.'

I searched the streets and back paddocks desperately for one child pull-along cart and its precious cargo, still placidly waiting her ride home.

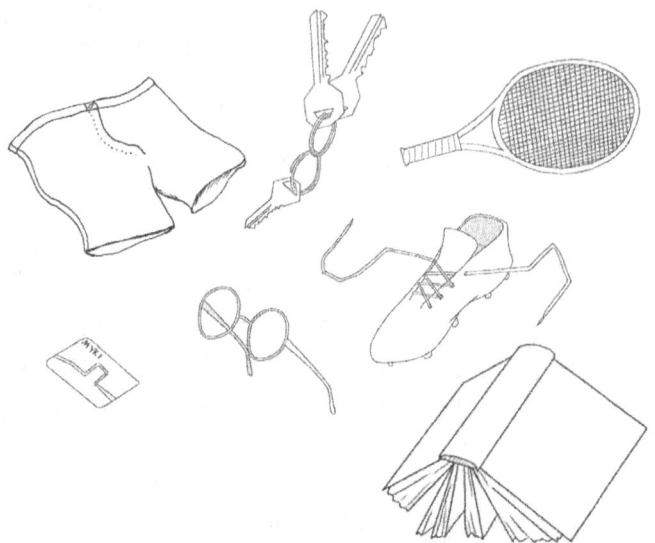

In due course, she grew old enough to mislay herself. She was always escorted by the dog, an oversize disapproving German shepherd. This was a mixed blessing, as no one ventured close enough to return her and worried well-wishers stood a respectful distance back to cajole and coax while the dog lifted a warning lip.

Naturally, by the time little girl number two could toddle, her bigger sister delighted in taking her for walks as soon as some unwary visitor left the gate unlatched. They went straight for the nearest main road or busy intersection, where they trotted along causing traffic to veer in all directions, and my heart to pound as I darted across the road to retrieve them.

By the time I had acquired a car, they were all old enough to lose car keys. Car keys had a certain mystique that appealed, or maybe it was the desperate appeals for their return. They were completely impartial: Mummy's keys, Daddy's keys, or any visitor's keys. Sometimes they ended down the toilet and sometimes stuffed into plastic scooters and toys, and sometimes they stayed missing forever.

Working on the system if you can't beat them you join them, I acquired dozens of key rings of disused keys for them. Apart from an odd panic when they mixed our keys with play keys, life settled down and breaking open locked doors and paying out for new keys and new ignition systems became an expensive memory.

By the time they started school, I was getting smug, but it was just the beginning. In the grey never-never land where lost things live, I spent years hunting.

My son lost lunches, football shorts, school trousers, cricket trousers, school ties, jumpers and blazers. Twice a year, he lost school bags and all his textbooks.

By the time I had graduated to chasing lost sewing and knitting, tennis racquets and hockey sticks, ballet slippers and odd raincoats, he had progressed to losing term tickets, yearly tickets, library tickets and his bike.

I spent most of my days roosting in the lost property depots at the schools and at the tramway, bus and railway offices.

There was a set pattern to losing thing. Term tickets were always lost in the first week of acquisition and yearly train tickets the day after buying them. I spent so much of my time chasing up JPs for signatures that my husband swore I was having an affair.

If the little girls lost books, they were always someone else's, borrowed against the retribution that awaits students who turn up at classes minus textbooks. Naturally, library books were always mislaid the day after they were due back.

They lost telephone numbers, letters before posting and their best friends. Sending any of them on errands risked them losing their way, my money or the shopping.

Inevitably, on their return from wherever they were sent, the conversations had a monotonous sameness to them.

'Well, I've got some bad news.' The hand rose to forestall the inevitable tirade. 'But I've got some good news too.

'Those shoes you sent me down to get repaired. I lost them, but I won a bottle of champagne.'

'You can't wear champagne.'

'So I walked to the station and saved one dollar on my bus fare.'

'I mislaid my term ticket, but I found those runners I mislaid on sports day.'

I went down to the depot for the school sewing. It arrived home, got carried back to school and left in the bus again. So I had to go down to the depot again and perhaps inquire about the three umbrellas that went missing on three consecutive wet days last week.

What puzzles me as a family of professional mislayers is what happens to all the odd gloves, socks, runners and football boots that get mislaid? They never turn up in the lost property depots. Are there a tribe of right- or left-footed bipeds to whom all the odd socks, runners, gloves and boots are sent? Shops are so unreasonable if you go in and ask to buy a right glove or a left football boot.

My eldest son is mislaying girlfriends and my eldest daughter is mislaying boyfriends. I refuse to take responsibility for them. My life is settling down to a spasmodic once-a-week visit to the lost property depots.

Right now, I appear to have mislaid my glasses, but I suppose they will turn up again.

First Words

'So clever,' doting man of the house marvelled. 'He's just said his first word, Daddy.'

'Daddy, Daddy, Daddy,' yelled the toddler, so proud of the admiration he caused.

So the favourite word got used full time.

However, travelling by public transport had its disadvantages.

'Daddy, Daddy, Daddy,' yelled the toddler at all the dark-haired men he spotted.

Some of them looked furtive and startled as they edged past, faces averted and shoulders bent.

Sad to realise it was not always a favourite word with some males.

The Collecting Instinct

Collecting is an odd instinct. Magpies and bowerbirds have it and most small boys. With small boys, it often matures through the years into the dignity of a hobby.

Magpies and bower birds stick to things that are brightly coloured and eye-catching. Young males begin, like magpies and bowerbirds, with coloured stones, graduate to marbles, then usually birds' eggs. By the time they have graduated to collecting birds of the two-legged variety, their mania for collecting usually fizzles out.

Sooner or later, the genuine collector collects a wife – always of a non-collector variety, and lives unhappily ever after. Wives develop into housewives and housewives become fanatic lifelong enemies of spiders and amassed junk. By the time the collector has collected a few kids, he is fighting an uphill battle.

I have been fascinated over the years by the antics of a genuine collector. The instinct to collect must be so deep and so compulsive that although it changes direction it never weakens.

Our genuine collector started off harmlessly by collecting stamps, until his kids, old enough to become literate, borrowed them for the practical purposes of use or swapping. He then industriously collected different brands of canned beer, until dear old Uncle Cedric, whose hobby was drinking, drank them all.

He then collected fancy bottles of expensive liquors. They decorated the back shelves of his cocktail cabinet, until his wife, during a financial emergency, discovered that they could be exchanged at the liquor stores for something practical like money and sold them.

The collector switched to collecting plastic model cars from packets

of breakfast cereals. As head of the household, it was acknowledged that he was entitled to have first choice of the packet. It was an innocuous hobby. He came home every night and soothed himself by having a little play with his toys, kept on the mantelpiece out of the destructive reach of the toddlers.

Unfortunately, while he was at work one day, a gang of nephews descended who just loved model cars, and cheap plastic didn't stand up too well to being raced around the lounge room. When he arrived home that night, he surveyed his dismembered cars mournfully and sighed.

Decimal currency arrived on the horizon. He decided to collect all the pre-decimal coinage still around. They filled the ideal criteria as collectibles. They were small enough to be hidden away, unbreakable and valuable enough to be kept out of the reach of sticky fingers. They piled up in a corner at the bottom of his wardrobe. He kept some of them in nice clear plastic sheets that he could take out and admire as they filled up.

He collected halfpennies and pennies, threepences, sixpences and florins, and the occasion sovereign. He paid out enormous sums of money for rare pennies and halfpennies. The larger grew his collection, the greater his pride.

Somehow the crunch came one night when he accepted the gift of a sticky chocolate from his smallest son, who was very generous in sharing with his dad.

'In the chips, son?' he enquired fondly.

'Yep,' agreed his small pride and joy.

'And who did you bite this time?' asked his sire.

'Cleaned up for you, Dad,' was the proud answer. 'And I found all these dirty old pennies, so I took them down to the shop and spent them.'

After this, the collector became discouraged. Especially when the lollyshop owner denied he had anything unusual in his cash register in the way of rare coins.

The collector, surrounded by his non-collector family, decided that the effort of collecting anything was too frustrating. To the best of my knowledge, all he ever collects nowadays are ulcers. Although, from the way he carried on for years, you would think he was the only person in the world who ever had a $600 1931 penny spent for what it was worth – a penny!

The Tomato Sauce Trick

I walked in on the confrontation. It was the usual mealtime battle of what food was not considered edible. The scowl was in full evidence.

My youngest and his mumps had been quarantined with grandmother. Grandmother hovered over the recovering convalescent.

He glared at his plate of stew. 'I do not eat stew,' he announced firmly. 'I don't like it.'

I inspected the rejected plate. Grandmother, being a great believer in good wholesome food, made rich old fashioned beef stew full of vegetables.

'But this isn't stew,' Grandmother said.

'It is,' contradicted the rebel.

'This is just meat pie without the pastry,' said Grandmother.

The tomato sauce got tipped over the spoonful of stew. The rebel gave the spoon heading towards his mouth a suspicious and disbelieving look. 'Really?'

'Tomato sauce on pie without the pastry,' Grandmother said. 'Taste it and see.'

The first spoonful was actually swallowed.

Then I watched an entire plate of good-quality nourishing stew being fed to the rebel without a single protest, all with the aid of tomato sauce and a terminological inexactitude.

Wish she had taught me that trick.

Heroes Never Kiss Girls

I hadn't realised that the days when cowboys kissed their horses and rode into the sunset at the end of a picture were gone.

The eight-year-old philosopher had been thinking, so we were having a discussion. The realistic technicolour blood and gore slaughter was being accepted as unblinking fact. It was his casual acceptance that actors should be prepared to carry their roles to the bitter end that shocked me.

'Do they use real actors?'

'Of course, but they don't really get killed, it's all just pretend.' I then explained at length that they used the same actors over and over again. If they killed them all off in the interests of realism, they wouldn't have any actors left.

He was not reassured. A very serious problem had undermined his enjoyment of cowboy pictures. 'Mum, the actors,' he scuffed his foot uneasily. 'They don't really kiss people, do they?'

I tried to remember what cowboy films he had watched. What hero would have feet of clay and betray a small boy's ideals and be sissy enough to kiss a girl?

'It's like them dying. It's just pretend.'

'It looked as if they were kissing.' He still wasn't convinced.

'Always looks like they are getting killed too.'

That was dismissed as unimportant.

I tried again. 'It's just the camera angle.'

'Didn't look like it.'

I appealed to his male logic. 'After all, a tough actor like that wouldn't really kiss a girl.'

I was rewarded with a relieved sigh.

'Suppose so.' But his voice still sounded accusing as he pondered the problem. 'But it did look as if he was kissing that girl.'

Adult Westerns have a lot to answer for!

Five Minutes in the Life of...

There was the high-pitched whine of racing gears, and Bikie Bill roared into the tiled bathroom. He idled back by the handbasin. The motor lowered to an ominous growl.

'And brush them properly.'

The engine noise rose to a crescendo, and then cut out.

Bikie Bill squinted at the mirror. Lips curled back in a snarl. One crooked tooth hung suspended and alone, its partner a wavy frill of enamel along the gum.

'And make sure you use your own toothbrush.'

Bikie Bill turned the tap on, and the steam billowed up around him, fogging the mirror. His reflection faded.

Dracula, the terror of the unborn dark formed from the shadows. Born anew to sap life and energy out of shrieking victims, leaving only the sound of blood drip drip dripping through the silence, and the weeping of the chosen.

It was a pleasing concept. He squirted a large teardrop across the glass with the toothpaste.

The bottom of the teardrop lengthened out into straggling whiskers. He rubbed two eyeholes in the steam. Bozo the clown stared back, bewildered and sad at his capture.

The bathroom tiles echoed to the drumming of his entrance into the circus rink. He used the toothpaste to outline a hat on his reflection, and pleased at his artistry, added the pompoms. 'Splot, splot, splot.'

The toothpaste tube 'oofed' as he pressed it again, and the blobs landed with unerring aim. They made a dead noise, like a gun with a silencer.

Dangerous Dan, the terror of the west, stared back at the levelled tube, gazing into the open jaws of death steady-eyed.

The Indians encircled the encampment, their horses thundering across the floor as they got closer.

Dangerous Dan pointed the tube with unerring aim. 'Splot, splot, you're dead!'

And the toothpaste bled down the mirror with the fallen bodies.

A dangerous man-eating python curved into deadly threat across the mirror, menacing towards him. Jungle Jim scowled as he throttled it with his bare hands.

This fight with the python left the map uncovered, a treasure trail across the trackless Amazon. A few dots marked the existence of the cannibals, outlining in the background, the high mountain peaks where the lost city hid.

A throttled shriek came from his throat. The plane was having trouble with the altitude! It was going to have to be a forced landing!

Down, down, down, swerving past the high jagged mountains, flattening into a glide as it came down into the mist-hung valley full of prehistoric monsters.

The shriek became a high-pitched scream through clenched jaws.

The plane spun crazily as it gathered speed. Biggles remained cool as he fought the controls.

The plane flattened out. Would he be able to dodge the brooding monsters in the swamp and pancake into the small beach? It all depended on his flying skill and cold-blooded daring.

The plane bounced. The floor echoed the impact as it rose again and gained height. It circled and dropped again. The undercarriage splintered as it landed heavily on the small beach by the man-eating vines.

The pilot tensed, ready to jump and start running as soon as the plane stopped moving.

'Will you hurry up and clean those teeth.'

Bikie Bill, alias, Dracula, alias Bozo the Clown, alias Dangerous Dan, alias Jungle Jim, alias Biggles and sometimes Fred the Pest, scowled and freckles and dirt screwed up towards resentful eyes.

'Gee, Mum! How can a fella clean his teeth without any toothpaste, huh?'

On Bathing Small Boys

I counted to ten and waited. The large plastic dome floated to the surface, spluttering like any whale.

'Did I stay under a full minute, Mum?'

'Certainly.' I reached out quickly before he submerged again.

Bathing small boys has its moments. Sometimes bathing with a friend is in. Having actually got him into the bath, I would return with clean pyjamas, to discover him joined by his current friend or friends.

The bathroom then became a threshing maelstrom of suds as they wrestled and fought. Under the strain, my floor tiles curled up like autumn leaves. My freshly set hair became in dire peril from the crossfire of the water pistols during the dash to battle stations.

For a while, the bath was considered an ideal place to practise dog-paddle, overarm and dead-man's-float.

If you are of a panicky turn of mind and you see a body motionless and face down, you are inclined to leap to the conclusion that there is a fatality in the family.

The passion for skin-diving was hard to take while it was popular. By the time the facemask and snorkel were in position, it was difficult to find areas of skin to wash, not to mention the marks that the rubber flippers made on the sides of the bath.

Then there was the craze for underwater battles. When the suds of conflict had been cleared, there were always dangerous rows of submarines and tanks lined up at the plughole, defended by the metal cannon.

There were always squeals from the unwary bathing after these battles. Some casualty of the fight, usually metal, was often overlooked, left to die with the rust stains oozing realistically down the centre of the bath.

Sometimes the bath was defended with last-ditch desperation from all comers, with a wooden stick spitting out bullets with machine gun rapidity.

For a while, astronauts were in and the bather, and all too often his friends, stepped into the bath wearing dedicated expressions and plastic motorbike helmets, the chinstraps making credible oxygen masks.

All this makes bath time that extra bit difficult. It is very hard to wash hair with a space helmet fastened down, and impossible to scrub knees hidden by a multitude of levers.

'Losing pressure,' he chanted as water swirled down the plug.

'Prepare for countdown,' friends intoned loudly, when forcibly removed from their space capsule, the bath.

I don't know where I get these antisocial tendencies and I know I haven't passed them on to the children, but I just can't approve of socialising in baths.

I just keep hoping that the bath can just be used for the purpose it was designed for, namely getting people clean.

The Worthy Cause

Betty Blue surveyed her garden gloomily. 'Absolutely cleaned out.'

There was a large strip of bald earth among her azaleas. I tutted in sympathy.

Betty Blue loved her garden and the soil was always wet and soft, so eager little fingers were able to pull out everything green within the given area.

'How much?'

'Five dollars, and the little horrors pulled out two azaleas and all the delphiniums.'

Not only does the hot sun of spring force up the weeds like hothouse plants, but it also brings out the enterprising young business-persons in the area.

There had been a continuous stream of them knocking on our doors, all eager to make their first million weeding gardens.

I surveyed my concrete hard ground. My plants were pretty safe. The workers had cleared a patch by the simple expedient of nipping off everything at ground level before vanishing with their undeserved five dollars.

This year, hard labour seemed to be in. There wasn't a single weed or plant safe in the entire district from the marauding bands of small boys and girls trying to earn an honest dollar.

The year before had been the age of the super salesperson. They sold everything from green plums pinched from my own tree, to broken pegs and packets of seed with no seeds in them.

The front door bell rang.

Two small boys and one small girl waited. 'Do any odd jobs for you?' they chorused.

'You can weed the sideway,' I said.

'Done,' said the spokesman smartly and ushered his helpers across to the driveway.

Ten minutes later, he rang the doorbell. I went out and inspected the damage. Most of the weeds and nearly all the geraniums had been broken off at ground level and placed in a high straggling pile on the path.

'Very good,' I said.

Three little faces lit up. I paid over three dollars blood money and they went on their way in a direct remorseless line towards Betty Blue.

I went inside. The front door bell went again. It was another wave of young hopefuls.

'Would you like to contribute towards a worthy cause?' asked the spokesperson.

'How worthy?' I asked.

The oldest brandished a card. It purported to authorise them to collect for the Explorer's Club that Saturday afternoon only, signature illegible.

'It sounds a worthy cause,' I said as I passed over my last one-dollar coin.

'We're saving up to go exploring.' The solemn-faced child was very earnest.

'Indeed, and where are you going exploring?' This sounded much more enterprising than the usual run of privateers.

'Oh, the show and other places of interest,' the gap-toothed boy said with a grin.

'Yeah, and Luna Park too,' the little girl with freckles chimed in.

They went off shaking their collection box happily.

The next time the door bell sounded, I peered through a crack in the door at the grubby little girl waiting. 'I'm not buying anything and I don't need any weeding done.'

She stared back at me out of shrewd blue eyes. 'I'm collecting bottles.'

'Beer bottles?' I brightened up. There was quite an accumulation behind our incinerator.

'No, money bottles.'

I led her around to the backyard. She tugged at three soft drink bottles from under the pile of beer bottles, gave me an absent nod and strolled off with them.

I looked at the tumbled pile of beer bottles, shrugged and went inside.

The doorbell went again.

Three little girls armed with books and pencils waited. 'Would you like to buy a raffle ticket…'

Pocket Money

'What about my pocket money?' The demand came like a bolt from the blue. My creditor watched me with accusing brown eyes.

'You haven't earned any.'

He breathed hard. 'I did the dishes twice and helped you make soup.'

'That's true.'

I had a new patent cutter and he had stood on a chair and thumped and thumped, spreading a generous carpet of diced vegetables over the sink, the stove and the floor.

'I'm supposed to get twenty-five cents a week and you didn't pay me for last week – that's fifty cents.'

'You found ten cents in the car park.'

'But that's not pocket money.'

'Nanna gave you twenty cents the other day.'

'That's still not pocket money. You give pocket money.' He started to get an injured note to his voice.

I hunted around for a way out. 'You said a bad word. Perhaps you shouldn't get pocket money this week.'

'But you did a bad thing to me.'

I felt a bit guilty. Perhaps washing a mouth out with soap wasn't a modern way of coping with *that* word.

I handed over fifty cents. 'What are you going to buy?'

'A can of meat soup.'

'You helped me make soup for dinner.'

'But I don't like your soup – I like tinned soup.'

'That soup costs seventy cents.'

He weighted up his fifty-cent piece and looked thoughtful. 'I've got a 1950 halfpenny – will that make it up?'

'It's not legal tender and the shop won't accept it.'

'Daddy has an 1841 halfpenny and it's worth a lot of money.'

'The shop won't accept your halfpenny,' I repeated.

He looked at his fifty-cent coin with the worries of the world on his brow, turned and left for his favourite place, the local supermarket.

Later, he rushed in as I was dishing up, clutching his packages. 'I bought you a delicious cake. You've got to eat it right now.'

'After dinner,' I promised.

'And I got a chocolate frog. I'm going to enter this competition. They are giving away bikes and cameras.'

'Fancy,' I marvelled.

He was a great enterer of competitions. He was always sending off grubby badly spelled envelopes with a touching faith in the unknown god of chance.

After dinner was over, I sat down with the cake and eyed it doubtfully.

'It's delicious. It's got apple inside.'

'You got a lot for your fifty cents.' I tried to procrastinate.

'They sold me the cake half-price 'cause it was stale and I kept it for you because you like apple cake.' He was full of simple pride at his own nobility.

I sipped my tea and nibbled the apple cake. He was right! It was stale!

'Do you like it?' He was starting to worry.

'Delicious,' I assured him and forced my way steadily through it.

His beaming face lightened my depression somewhat, but the administration of pocket money places a heavy load on my digestive system.

The Tooth Fairy

The argument went on and on. Father Christmas was discounted with other childish beliefs.

'What about the Easter Bunny?'

'That's different. The Easter Bunny never comes to kids who don't believe in him, so I intend to believe in him forever.'

'What about the Tooth Fairy?'

'I know there is such a thing as the Tooth Fairy.' He grinned, showing the wavy frill of his new teeth with his smile. 'My baby teeth have always turned into dollar coins when I leave them in the glass overnight.'

I did wonder about the man of the house always paying out so freely for the discarded teeth. What did he ever intend to do with them?

'Now you're grown all your new teeth, she won't come any more for you.'

The sceptic looked horrified. 'How long will it be before my new second teeth fall out?'

'They should last you the rest of your life, especially now you haven't got any Tooth Fairy money to waste on sweets,' I explained.

He scowled and stamped off. For some reason, this was not good news.

He arrived back later in the afternoon with blood pouring from his nose and a black eyes.

'You've been fighting again,' I accused.

'Only with my best friend,'

'So that makes it all right?' I asked.

'I pushed him and he pushed me back. I kicked him and he kicked me back. He punched me and I punched him back.'

He sounded triumphant. Had he won the fight with his best friend?

That night there was a glass of water beside his bed. There was also a tooth in it.

'Enterprising,' said the man of the house. 'Waiting for the tooth fairy with someone else's tooth.'

'It's his best friend's,' I said. 'They had a fight.'

The tooth was left in lonely splendour in the glass for several days.

'That's it!' the sceptic grumbled at last. 'I don't believe in the Tooth Fairy.'

'The Tooth Fairy isn't going to pay you for a tooth that isn't yours. Perhaps you had better give it back.'

'Seeing as how he is my best friend, I will give it back.'

The next day I glared with disapproval at the tooth-rotting collection of sweets he arrived home with.

'The tooth fairy changed my best friend's tooth for a whole two dollars and we shared,' explained the sceptic. 'And it just proves there is really such a thing as the Tooth Fairy.'

The Class Raffle

It was a pretty kitten, with distinctive ginger and white markings. Unconscious of my dislike, it purred loudly, milk droplets still on its whiskers.

'We already have a cat and we don't need another one, especially a female. Return it.'

'It's so beautiful,' said my daughter tearfully. 'Why doesn't anyone like dear little kittens?'

'It's not going anywhere,' said my determined son. 'I paid twenty cents for a raffle ticket. The whole class went in that raffle and I won it.'

'I'll find another home for it,' I suggested. 'A good home where it will be looked after.'

Putting the kitten under my arm, I stalked over the road to visit Betty Blue. To the best of my knowledge, she didn't own a cat, but I felt sure she would be tolerant of another mouth to feed.

'My, my,' she uttered when she saw the kitten.

'A present for you,' I smiled.

'And a present for you,' she said, baring her teeth at me. She scooped up a kitten with the same ginger and white markings. 'My daughter won it in a raffle at school.'

'If you'll mind my kitten,' I said. 'I'll take a walk around the neighbourhood.'

Betty Blue produced a birdcage and stuffed the kittens inside. 'I'll take a walk with you.'

We were footsore and tired by the time we got back and collapsed at the kitchen table to drink tea.

Betty Blue was calculating on the edge of her shopping list. 'Forty kids in the class, all buying at least one raffle ticket at twenty cents each.'

'Eight dollars.' I was impressed. 'Not to mention what he collected from the other classes.'

'Not bad, you know,' Betty Blue said as she studied the caged kittens. 'He's obeyed his mother's orders to dispose of a litter of eight ginger kittens – and made a profit on the deal.'

'Future prime minister material,' I agreed mournfully.

It was a great comfort to me to realise that there were seven other mothers in the district faced with the identical problem of ridding their homes of one ginger and white striped kitten won by their offspring in a raffle.

Home Nursing

I pulled out the oven tray slowly. There was a very dead white mouse on it. This was the third mouse that had got roasted in my oven this week, due to the 'keep the pet warm' system of medical care.

I turned off the oven.

'What are you doing with my mouse?' accused a voice behind me.

'Taking it out of the oven.'

'But it's dead!' My daughter's voice held a rising note of grief and disappointment.

'They don't seem to like being roasted.'

'But I only put it in to keep it warm.'

I tipped the corpse on to a newspaper and put some water on to boil to sterilise my oven tray. 'Bury it.'

I was ignored. The *How to Take Care of Your Pets* bible was being studied carefully.

'Can't imagine why I'm losing so many animals. That's three mice and two guinea pigs this week.'

I had difficulty controlling my elation. At this rate, we could be a pet-free household by the end of winter.

'They're all getting pneumonia.' She gave me an accusing stare.

I stared back. Sick pets were allowed inside for doctoring but I fought a bitter and losing battle against the infiltration of pets as permanent residents in my house. Night after night, I hunted down and dragged white mice, guinea pigs and the occasional rabbit from their places of concealment and ordered them outside.

This evening, Mopsy the white rabbit was in the place of honour by the heater. He arched his head back and shuddered as he scrabbled in front of him with nervous front paws.

'What's wrong with him?'
'I think it's pneumonia and my book said to give him some spirits.'
'What spirits?'
'There was an old bottle of rum at the back of the cupboard.'

The rabbit arched back in another uncontrollable spasm. I couldn't take my eyes off him as he lurched and staggered around the box to his riotous inevitable alcoholic poisoning end. One thing was certain: Mopsy would never pass a breathalyser test.

'How much rum?'
'Only two tablespoons.'

Her brother was disgusted. It was his job to bury deceased pets and his sympathy had long since been strained to breaking point. 'Suppose they are dying happy, but what about trying smaller doses next time?'

The next evening, a fluffy guinea pig was in the place of honour by the heater, jerking and scrabbling with beady eyes blinking, until its last back-arching convulsive end.

'At least they're dying happy,' said the chief undertaker. 'How much rum this time?'

'Just two teaspoons.' My daughter was still tearful. 'I can't understand why they aren't recovering.'

I studied the shoebox (official hospital ward) the following evening. Its occupant was the last white mouse. A large handsome animal as mice went, with beady pink eyes and a long pink tail. 'Has he got pneumonia too?'

At this rate, she was doing a better job than the Pied Piper and with the best of intentions.

'Yes.'

Marmaduke fixed me with a cunning pink eye and scuttled in an unsteady figure of eight around the box.

'What dosage is he having?'

The eyedropper was waved under my nose. 'Just the cooking sherry, Mum. I knew you wouldn't mind. Look how lively he is.'

Marmaduke increased his erratic circuit of the box. Around and around and backwards and forwards he went, pink tail flicking as he scrabbled at the corners

'We ought to race him,' marvelled the undertaker. With the last funeral, he had worked himself out of a job, so he could afford to be tolerant.

The next morning, Marmaduke wasn't so lively. He spared me a glance out of dulled pink eyes as he crawled into the darkest corner of the box. His fur was lank and unhealthy and his tail dragged lifelessly behind him.

'Classic symptoms of a hangover,' pronounced the ex-undertaker, giving a quick inspection before going to school.

'He just needs more medicine to liven him up,' his owner said confidently.

My head twinged in sympathy with Marmaduke. It must have been awful to be introduced to the demon drink in the full flush of pneumonia and then be forced to ingest more drink while still hung over.

The credit for Marmaduke's recovery was generously acknowledged to the *How to Take Care of Your Pets* book.

Marmaduke took eagerly to his drop of the doings every night and lived his short life to the full.

He spent his nights running in wild and erratic circles and his days unsociably in the darkest corner of his cage. His pink eyes grew blurred and his nose bulbous. His proud owner declared frequently that he had never looked more handsome.

To my mind, his face had a shifty expression on it, but I suppose you couldn't expect too high a character of the only alcoholic mouse in captivity.

The Problem With Crackers

A swarm of small boys played with crackers on the vacant allotment. One of them was familiar.

'Time for dinner,' I said as I raced over and grabbed him.

'Don't hold my arm,' he grumbled. 'Everyone will see.'

'Whose crackers?'

'Mine.'

'Where did you get the money to buy crackers?'

'I just helped myself to next week's pocket money from your purse.' Injured note in his voice. 'It was still my pocket money.'

'Who bought them for you?'

Local rules were that nobody under twelve years of age can be sold crackers.

'A friend.'

'What's his name?'

'Didn't ask. He was just a friend I met.'

'I'll buy the crackers back off you.'

'That's not fair. They're my crackers.'

'They're dangerous.'

'Not to little boys who let them off properly.'

'*All* little boys.'

'Gee, I'm not an idiot. I'm very careful.'

'Some naughty little boys let them off in tins and bottles and it's very dangerous.'

'Gee, Mum. When I let them off in bottles, I always run very fast so the broken glass doesn't catch me.'

I tried to stay civilised. 'Some little boys lose their eyes playing those sorts of games.'

'I wouldn't. I'm very careful.'

I realised the futility of being reasonable and civilised. 'Hand over the crackers and the matches.'

'Can't I let off just one more? It's great fun.'

'No.'

'I can go up in the pine trees where nobody will hear.'

I thought of the tinder-dry undergrowth around the pine trees and shuddered. Little boys with matches and crackers during a long hot summer were an uncool combination.

I tucked the crackers and the matches in my apron pocket. The discussion was over.

'You're always spoiling my fun. I hate you,' he sobbed as he retired defeated.

I disposed of the crackers and grimly wished for the name of the helpful friend who had bought them.

A Money Problem

'Money is a problem,' my daughter said with a sigh.

'Well, you should have plenty.' I was tart. Generous relations had showered her with money for Christmas.

'I'm broke!'

'What did you do with it all?'

'Brought Christmas presents.'

This was said with great dignity. After all, she had remembered the whole family when she bought Christmas presents.

'You received another ten dollars yesterday and Christmas is over.'

'I just had to buy another Christmas present.'

'Who for?' I couldn't remember anyone she had forgotten in her generous Christmas spending spree.

She had the grace to look sheepish. 'Myself! I forgot to buy anything for me!'

'So what did you buy?'

'I'll show you when the time is suitable.' She sounded evasive and a bit nervous. 'You'll probably say it's an extravagance.'

'I would say that anyway.

I returned to cooking dinner. It is a waste of time, but I often wonder what she gets taught at school under the subject name of economics?

A Business Enterprise

I was temporarily puzzled by the visitor at the front door until I spotted a son lurking in the background.

'I saw this small kid struggling to shift this cage bigger than himself and thought he deserved a lift,' the visitor said expansively. 'So I brought him and his cage home.'

'So kind,' I muttered.

The visitor took off. I inspected the enormous cage that my son had found. Too big for a guinea pig or chook cage, too small for a pony stall, and goats weren't kept in cages. What sort of animal was a cage that big going to fit? Hopefully, there were no stray lions or tigers around the Australian bush.

'Me and my friend have decided to breed pigeons,' my son volunteered.

I glared suspiciously at his best friend, a red-haired kid with a cheeky grin and an amoral attitude to all adult rules and regulations. I could see him breeding ferrets, feral cats, snakes and poisonous wasps, but definitely not pigeons.

'It's a very large cage,' I said.

'We've been reading up on homing pigeons,' I was informed. 'Need a large cage for pigeons.'

I cheered up. Pigeons were inoffensive and must be a lot cheaper to feed than some of the other animals, birds and reptiles that lived so contentedly in my apology for a back garden.

The cage was put on legs, a waterproof cover thrown over the top, and then as the finances of part-time jobs and parental donations arrived, so did the pigeons, more and more of them. I started to worry about the overcrowding in the cage. It looked like bird cruelty to me.

'They need to be kept locked up until they know that this is their home,' I was informed. 'And they're happy because they're now a flock.'

To my surprise and deep suspicion, the pigeons were kept expensively fed and watered and the cage cleaned, if not the ground beneath them.

I started to get worried at the continued unnatural dedication of the two small boys to the cleaning and feeding and care of the new pets. They seemed very uninteresting pets for two entrepreneurs.

Three weeks later, I went out to check what was happening. The pigeons had been homed satisfactorily, I was informed, and were going to be allowed out for their first flight.

The doors were opened. The flock of pigeons rose swept up in the sky and circled our yard.

'Home, home, you beauties,' the two small boys screamed, jumping up and down and swinging their arms.

The flock of pigeons circled gracefully one more time a lot higher up and vanished into the blue yonder. They did not return.

'And we were going to make so much money out of them,' my son mourned.

'How? I asked.

'When they homed, we were gonna be able to keep reselling them,' the red-haired villain of the district explained.

'What a cheat that pet shop owner was,' muttered my son. 'Selling us homing pigeons that didn't home.'

I returned inside, thankful for the collapse of the pigeon business enterprise.

School lunches

'What do you want on your sandwiches?'

The morning rush was in full swing.

'What is there?'

'Peanut butter, Vegemite and pork sausage.'

'Yes.'

'Which?'

'The lot,' ordered my eldest, whose lunch was always the heaviest part of his schoolbag.

'Spread the Vegemite thickly,' urged my Vegemite-hater.

'But you don't like Vegemite.'

'I swap it with Patsy.'

'What does Patsy's mother give her?'

'Ham sandwiches. Patsy hates ham sandwiches.' She screwed up her nose at Patsy's mother, who cut nothing else but ham sandwiches.

'So why doesn't Patsy's mother give her something else?'

Eyebrows went up in surprise. 'Because Patsy likes to swap for my Vegemite sandwiches and I love ham sandwiches.'

I concentrated on the family dieter. The weeks her midriff bulged, she had fast days. I couldn't remember whether this was a cut-down-on-calories week. 'What do you want for lunch?'

'Just peanut cookies.'

'You told me you were sick of peanut cookies.'

'So! The girls are mad on your peanut cookies. Two of them are equal to a chocolate éclair, and for three I get a bottle of Coke.'

'A very well balanced diet.'

'Well, I have to watch what I eat, you know.'

'So what do you want on your sandwiches?'

She drew herself upright, flattening her stomach with a conscious effort. 'You don't expect me to eat anything fattening like bread, do you? You know I have to watch my diet.'

I spread tomato sauce on pork sausage sandwiches for my youngest, a solid citizen if ever there was one.

'Spread it out to the corners, Mum.'

I spread it out to the corners.

'Now cut off the crusts.'

'Waste of sauce,' I grumbled.

'Now cut it into four like party sandwiches.'

'That makes very tiny sandwiches.'

'I like tiny sandwiches. Besides, I'm not hungry.'

'But you will be by lunchtime.'

This argument went on every morning at sandwich-cutting time.

'No, I won't.' He was adamant. 'Can I have an apple?'

I beamed approval. It was nice to have at least one member of the family eating fruit. 'Remember to chew it properly.'

'It's not for me. It's for my friend.'

'Which friend?'

'Rollick.'

I looked blank.

'I meet him every morning for a talk.'

'That's nice.'

The gang of little boys my son ran around with were all doers and not noted for quiet discussion groups. I tried to remember which one might be a talker.

'In the paddock next to the school,' he prompted.

'The horse!'

'Yeah. See you, Mum.'

The door banged behind him, while I seriously pondered the futility of cut lunches.

After-school Games

School was out. Three small boys kicked a football around the yard. They paused in their play. There was a brief discussion, and then they drifted off. Soon the hum of their voices came faintly from the far paddock.

I put a cushion on the step and relaxed in the sun with a book.

'Mum!' It sounded like high drama as one small boy came racing up. 'Quick! I've set the paddock on fire!'

The black smoke billowed up. There was the convincing crackle of tinder-dry grass and bushes. I sprinted for the hose and the tap. In my haste, I couldn't get the hose connection on the thread properly.

'Who's been playing with matches?'

'He did!' One small boy pointed to another.

'They weren't my matches. He lit them.' The accused pointed to another small boy.

'But they were your crackers I threw.' The logic was unassailable.

I opened my mouth to argue and then shut up. There just wasn't time. The fire was gaining with alarming rapidity and racing straight for the pine trees.

'Gee, it's a good fire,' said one small boy.

I got the hose connection on straight at last despite my shaking hands, turned the tap full on, picked up the hose and ran across the paddock.

There were three individual fires. The smoke billowed up more thickly as the flames subsided with sulky hisses.

The boys hovered around disappointed.

'It went out quick.' There was a wistful tone to the remark.

'How come?' I asked. 'Three separate fires started?'

'We were throwing crackers,' my son explained.

'You aren't allowed to let off crackers without supervision,' my voice rose. 'And then only in the car park.'

'We thought if we were a long way away, the noise wouldn't worry you.' My son watched me out of the corner of one eye.

I restrained myself with an effort.

'We did ask if we could let them off, but you mightn't have heard us.'

'No, I might not have heard you.' I put out one hand. 'Hand them over.'

Three little boys emptied out pockets and watched glumly as the crackers were thrown into the bin.

'And my matches?'

There were blank stares. I searched three sets of pockets and checked the grass.

'Sorry, I lost them, Mum.'

'Yeah.' Another small boy spoke up. 'Anyway, we found four soft drink bottles in the long grass. We can buy you some more matches.'

Three small boys carrying four soft drink bottles sauntered towards the shops.

There was a pause as they sampled unripe plums from a tree, and then vanished around the corner of the house.

I returned to my cushion in the sun and tried to relax again.

The School Dance

There was the usual last-minute indecision. The rope of wooden beads or the pearl pendant; the two-tone mauve shoes or the Roman sandals?

She at last swept into the car in a potpourri of Opium, baby talc, cologne and skin freshener. 'I'll ring if I don't get a lift home.'

'Ring anyway. I don't know why the schools run mid-week dances.'

'I'm fifteen. A late night won't kill me.'

She rang later, yelling through the ear piece of a public phone. 'Got a lift with…crackle…crackle…'

'What's wrong with your phone?'

'Flat battery!' she yelled back.

'Who did you say you got a lift with?' but she had hung up.

I went to bed and relaxed. At least I didn't have to go out again to collect her.

By midnight, I was no longer relaxed. I got dressed and prowled the house worrying.

If the dance finished at eleven-thirty and it was only twenty minutes' drive home, where was she?

Half an hour later, I stood out the front jangling my car keys and still worrying. The dog came out to stare at me. The cats tucked themselves beside me and waited.

Who did she say she was coming home with? Which girlfriend did she say she was actually going to meet at the dance? Was it too late to ring someone's mother?

The road was dark and the night peaceful. Only I wasn't at peace! No headlights flashed over the hill towards our house.

Was she coming home with the boy who rang earlier in the evening

to check if she was going to the dance? Was he a P-plater? Did he drink? Was his car a mangled wreck at the bad intersection? I jangled my keys again. I should have insisted to picking her up!

Was she sitting in a pizza parlour eating a substantial supper, flirting and giggling – forgetting she had promised to come straight home? Was she sitting in a parked car listening to the inevitable proposition with wide-eyed interest? Such a brand-new proposition to a brand-new female.

The street stayed dark. Was it about time I had a belated talk about some of the messier facts of life? Kids seemed so knowing. Was it just a facade?

I went back inside and looked at the clock. It was one a.m. Should I start ringing the casualty sections of the hospitals? Should I ring the police? If only I had caught the name of who was bringing her home!

I went outside again. Headlights came down the hill, paused and turned into the driveway.

A big smile glowing in the reflection from the dashboard. Dark figures jostling around so she could get out.

'What are you doing still up?' she asked in surprise.

'Past your curfew,' I snarled.

The car backed out of the driveway to chorused farewells.

'Gee. Mum, all the rest of the kids had to be dropped first. John's dad must've driven home the whole mob.'

I pulled my clothes off and fell into bed. I woke again later to realise her light was still on. She was still fully dressed, sitting on her bed, contemplating her sandals with a dreamy smile.

'Get to bed.'

'Gee. Mum, I was just thinking.'

I turned out her light, left her to get undressed in the dark and stomped back to bed. It was exactly two a.m. I just can't take late nights like a fifteen-year-old.

The New Pet

I was puzzled as I shot into the bedroom to break up the latest fight between the pet lover and my youngest son. So he had arrived with a new pet. Why was his sister against yet another pet in the house?

My youngest son was usually into birds and even went to school with tamed birds perched on his shoulder. At the moment, his current bird was outside twittering hysterically on the fence.

His sister was screaming, 'It is not living in the house. I'm going to ring the police, the RSPCA and the zoo.'

'You sneak in your mice, guinea pigs, baby possums, rabbits and stray cats,' he accused. 'It's too delicate to leave out in the cold.'

'So what is it?' I asked.

His doona got flung back dramatically. A smallish snake rested on his electric blanket. It raised a languid head and looked at us.

'It's not a whitelips,' his sister screamed. 'It'is an ordinary venomous brown snake that has just shed a skin. You want to kill us all.'

'I paid out good money for it at the pet shop,' her brother snarled. 'You're the idiot who doesn't know the difference between whitelips non-venomous and brown snakes which are protected anyway.'

'So what do they eat?' the pet lover demanded suspiciously.

'I can keep it, can't I, Mum?' he pleaded. 'It won't be any trouble. Snakes are quiet and house-trained and cheap to feed.'

I wasn't game to bring up how cheap his snake could be to feed. The pet-loving sister still had white mice and I worried that the knowledge of the cheap diet for the new pet might cause more tantrums. (I don't think I would have been so tolerant if I had discovered back then that he was feeding his new pet his sister's white mice.)

When his older brother went through the snake stage, he was busy saving up for a python. As pythons then cost a dollar a foot, it was taking him a while to save the required amount for his required length. When he had enough money for his longed-for purchase, he only then checked into its required diet.

'One live white mouse a week,' I reported.

As he was going through his white mice for pets stage, he then lost interest in buying his python.

'I suppose it can stay if it really is a whitelips,' I decided.

'It's a brown snake,' his sister repeated.

The new pet was in residence for a fortnight. I wasn't game to ask what it was fed during that time. A very temping price was offered by another snake lover and it went.

It had been a peaceful fortnight. No other pets were sneaked into the house, regardless of how cold the nights got. Everyone was subdued, quiet and abnormally tidy about putting away their shoes.

And I have to admit that the snake's permanent home on the electric blanket did discourage me from changing that bed for the fortnight.

Like the pet lover, I didn't know the coloration difference between a whitelips and a brown snake.

The Cooking Disaster

The smell of burnt cake and gloom hung heavily over the kitchen. I inspected the disaster. The centre had plunged and the sides climbed steeply. The cake was pitted and scarred like a moon crater.

'Perhaps we could buy a cake?'

'Mum! We've got to make them! It's for cooking!'

'Well, cook another one at school.'

'We've got to make them at home! We're going to learn how to ice them tomorrow.'

The situation called for drastic measures. That dramatic flamboyant flop had cost ten dollars for ingredients, not counting the sweet sherry that had been sloshed through with a free hand.

'You can make a boiled fruit cake,' I said. 'They are foolproof.'

She floundered around, spilling sugar, flour and dried fruit over the floor. She stood poised over the saucepan, wooden spoon at the ready. 'Mrs Gofoops doesn't do it this way.'

'We're doing it *my* way. Keep stirring.'

The ingredients at last got as far as the cake tin. She scooped out the centre and piled it up against the sides. It looked like becoming moon crater number two.

'What do you think you're doing?'

'Mrs Gofoops told us to do it this way, so it doesn't rise in the middle.'

I crashed the tin down, and the mixture levelled off again.

'But Mum, it's got to be flat, otherwise I can't ice it.'

I forcibly took the tin off her and put it in the oven.

'But Mum, they're supposed to be cooked second shelf down. Nobody cooks cake on the top shelf.'

'I do,' I snarled. 'And my cakes turn out all right.'

Peace descended on the kitchen for ten minutes. I relaxed. With a foolproof recipe like the boiled fruit cake one, nothing could go wrong.

'What are you opening the oven for?' I heard my voice rising to an eldritch screech.

'Don't yell! I'm just having a look.'

'You never open an oven door after you've put a cake in.'

'I thought that was just for sponge cakes. Don't yell, Mum. You're giving me earache.'

I came back an hour later. The kitchen was clean and she sat reading.

'How's the cake?'

'All right, I suppose.'

'You suppose! Haven't you checked?'

'The hour was up, so I just turned the oven off.'

I rushed to investigate. The cake looked cooked. I didn't have sufficient courage to test it with a skewer.

'It rose a lot.' She sounded discontented. 'Told you I should have made a hollow in the centre.' There was silence for a few seconds as she studied it. 'I can turn it upside down while it's still soft so the hill sinks back into the middle.'

'Definitely not!' I felt myself go white.

'It looks like Mount Everest! I can't ice it like that.'

'See what Mrs Gofoops suggests.' I was losing interest. Nobody ever complained before about my cakes rising.

'I've got to have a flat surface.' The tears were getting closer to the surface. 'I'm going to do a green deer outlined in silver.'

I studied the beautifully rounded top of the cake. It seemed a pity to desecrate it with a green deer outlined in silver. 'Can't you just practise on cardboard?'

'Mum! We've got to ice a cake for cooking.'

I felt myself breathing heavily as I reached for the meat saw.

'But Mum, you're not supposed to cut them. Mrs Gofoops says…'

'Don't tell her. Is this flat enough?'

'Guess so.'

The fruit cake with the flat sawn-off top went to school and I waited for the report.

'My decorating was okay, but Mrs Gofoops says the cake wouldn't keep as well as the other recipe.'

'I make my cakes to eat, not look at.'

'What are you so touchy about, Mum? Gee, I'm the one who made it.'

Relationships

Just lately, I have been having trouble with relationships.

'I hate her,' stormed my youngest daughter.

'Who?'

'Patsy.'

'Isn't she your best friend?'

'Of course she is. She's a pig!'

'Well, don't play with her.'

'Don't play with my best friend!.' I received an incredulous look. 'You mad or something? My best friend!'

I changed the subject. 'I believe Fay Fluffyhead has been expelled.'

'Yeah.'

'Did you hear why?'

Fay Fluffyhead had been a thorn in the side of law and order for several terms.

'Oh, she got engaged.' This really was scandal!

'Who did she get engaged to?'

'I dunno. Some friend of hers.'

I gave up and went to check on my littlest male. A stable character if ever there was one.

'Where are you going?'

'Round to Billy's.'

'I thought you said Billy was a sooky baby?'

'He is, but I've got to play with someone.' This was delivered reproachfully.

'Well, give me a kiss before you go.'

He was shocked, but relented. 'Come round the corner where no one will see and I'll give you a hug.'

I checked up on my other daughter. She was painting her toenails bright blue.

'Are you going out with George?'

'Hardly.'

'What's wrong with George?' He had seemed a nice boy, but then you never can tell.

'I've been out with him twice.'

'So?'

'If I go out with him again, I'm going steady.' She shuddered at the thought. 'Fancy going steady and he's practically middle-aged!'

'How old?'

'At least eighteen.'

'Well, where are you going?'

'Down the club.'

'What's down the club?'

'Boys.'

'Middle-aged ones?' I was starting to get confused.

'There might be somebody interesting down there.'

'To go out with?'

'No.' She condescended to explain. 'If you go out with them, you aren't free to meet them.'

I gave up.

My youngest daughter was just off the phone. She was radiant. 'Mum. I'm going skating with Sherry Sharptongue.'

'You told me she was your worst enemy.' I had heard dark tales of unfair rivalry right through the school year.

My daughter became impatient at my stupidity. 'Really, Mum, what does that matter? We're going skating together. You don't expect me to let a little matter like hating someone interfere with an afternoon's ice-skating!'

'No,' I agreed meekly.

'You're always asking silly questions. I hate people who ask silly questions all the time!'

The Delicate Problem

'Mum! I've got problems!' He slouched in gloomily, throwing his school-bag down with a thump, and sprawled on the chair.

I kept a sharp eye on the plate of cakes I had just finished icing. 'Haven't we all?'

He swallowed two cakes and sighed heavily. 'It's about my education.'

They had been having lectures on jobs and careers that week. Perhaps I was going to hear something positive.

'Well,' I prompted as I shifted the cakes out of danger.

He reached long arm over for another cake and munched thoughtfully. 'It's about sex!'

I shifted the cakes further out of reach. 'Discuss it with your father.'

'I can't discuss anything with Dad.'

I thought that statement over. For once, he was right! These days, their conversations seemed to be limited to saying goodbye to each other's departing back.

'I thought you learned all that sort of thing at school?'

'Oh yeah! I've been discussing it with the gang. At school, all the teachers assume you're taught at home, and at home all the parents assume the teachers get around to it.'

'I thought you knew all about biology?' I was puzzled. His marks were always satisfactory.

'It's not the biology, it's just – relationships.'

'I hope you're not letting yourself get dragged behind the bushes by some of those high school brats in the name of education?'

I was suddenly suspicious and unsympathetic. Some of the teenagers in our locality were enthusiastically amoral by our more square adult standards and occasionally the whole district resounded to scandal.

'I would struggle, kicking and screaming all the way,' he said wistfully.

I flapped the tablecloth over the table and braced myself. 'Just exactly what do you want to know?'

'Must be books on the subject, Mum?'

I relaxed. This was an easier solution than I had been expecting. Of course there were books on the subject! How much easier it made life to be literate.

The next day, I got directed into the right department and spent my precious lunch hour in an agony of indecision. I'll say there were books on the subject! Even narrowed down to the correct age group, there were still volumes and volumes, all purporting to tell the right and correct things about relationships, sex and budgeting.

I kept browsing. Some were written in an arch, twee manner; some were very moral and some were patronising; while others bogged down in a welter of sticky sentimentality. Some books were odiously righteous, and would have made suitable reading to mentally retarded children by simple-minded spinsters.

In desperation, I picked two books that looked reasonably adult and sensible. One was on psychological relationships with teens and the other on sex and the single student. I covered them in brown paper and handed them over.

They were accepted graciously and the dread subject dropped its ugly head for a few days.

'Aren't there other books, Mum?'

'Did you happen by any chance to want the *Kama Sutra* or perhaps something on the techniques on love-making?' I asked, trying sarcasm to get him to drop the subject.

'That's it, Mum – just what I want!' His face brightened up at my sudden ability to home in on his wavelength!

'At sixteen?' I snarled, not at all flattered. 'That knowledge shouldn't be indispensable.'

'Well, you're neglecting my education,' he said gloomily. 'I've been talking with the fellas and someone said there are thirty-four positions.'

I glared at him. I tried not to let my bottom jaw drop.

He didn't notice. He had an aggrieved tone to his voice. 'And we can all only work out twenty-two!'

The Casualty

Tragedy had struck! Our mainly boxer dog Buffo had walked into the path of a speeding car. A hit and run menace who hadn't even slowed after the incident.

'See how white and shaken he is,' said one daughter, who tended to dramatise.

I wasn't sure that a dog could be white and shaken, but I was prepared to concede a point. The dog seemed shaky and the side of his head was matted with blood. Even the lightest handling of his head and ear caused piteous yelps of pain.

'Could be ear damage,' worried her sister.

'Or a fractured skull,' predicted her brother.

'Or brain damage,' moaned the dramatist.

Buffo's mournful eyes went from one to the other of his audience. He realised the gravity of the situation. With a lot of petting and coaxing, he permitted us to cleanse the blood from his head and mangled ear, being brave and noble about the entire unpleasant business.

After that was over, he limped over and waited by the fridge. His one alert ear had an expectant angle. Accidents come and go, but he was due to be fed. I tried him on a small piece of meat loaf. He carried it over to the corner of the yard and tried to bite. It fell out of his mouth. He sat and looked at me.

I cut it into smaller cubes. He ate it slowly, being careful not to put any pressure on his jaws. This was worrying. Lack of appetite had to be checked out. He limped after us, and waited to be helped into the car, resignation and devotion written all over him. He made it obvious he would rather repair his shattered nerves and broken bones in the peace and quietness of the house, but he knew his duty. Family came first, despite serious injuries.

He was happy to visit, but it wasn't until he was swung up on the stainless steel bench that it dawned on him where he was. He took one look at the shining metal torch the vet held and transformed into a cringing struggling coward, remembering all those nasty injections that he had suffered on this very bench.

It took four of us to hold him down. He burrowed his nose against my shoulder as the vet lifted his ear.

'No damage, just a mangled flap,' the vet reported.

Buffo sat up. He was visibly relieved. One ear came forward. You could almost see him begin to breathe again.

'About his jaw?'

Buffo obligingly opened wide, exposing gleaming back teeth and long pink tongue.

The vet probed along the line of jaw, his head nearly in Buffo's mouth. 'Just bruised muscle, no damage.' The vet patted him.

Buffo quivered with pleasure. He enjoyed being the centre of attention.

'No damage!' I repeated. I fixed Buffo with an unkind eye. He had the grace to look ashamed. 'What about his limp?'

'Pure fraud.' The vet lifted Buffo down from the bench.

We left. Buffo headed for the car. His head was held high with one ear cocked forward. There was not a trace of a limp in his buoyant trot. His tail waved in its usual satisfied manner.

'Fraud!' I snarled.

Buffo pretended not to hear, gazing with noble disdain out the car window.

When we arrived home, he waited hopefully by the fridge. I presented him with a full meat loaf. He gave me a reproachful gaze. It was a game I wasn't playing.

'If you can't chew it, starve,' I said and went inside.

With what looked like a resigned shrug, Buffo picked up the meatloaf and tossed it into the air, catching it in strong jaws and biting through powerfully and smoothly. His recovery from both accident and attitude seemed complete!

The Intelligent Solution

My son had just become one of the five Year-Twelve boys appointed as prefects. I listened with respect to their tasks. They were now the lords of creation with their own brand-new carpeted study and almost the power of life and death over the underlings. They were expected to use their power in an intelligent, logical and just manner.

They had to make sure the college standards of dress code and behaviour were kept up, so they inspected uniforms and prowled the public transport the students used for lapses of correct behavior.

'He swallowed his cigarette so he wouldn't be caught smoking on the train,' my son explained. 'A grubby little kid, too young to smoke anyway.'

'A live cigarette?' I asked.

'Yeah. His claim to fame around the school,' my son explained.

An adopted kitten was smuggled into the brand-new carpeted study. They were studying why kittens were playful, so it came under the heading of science. There was an accident on the new carpet.

'Didn't know kittens could have diarrhoea just like people,' my son mused.

'Did you manage to get the carpet clean again?' I asked.

'We're studying the problem,' my son said evasively.

And the problem kept on being studied without any actual cleaning being done.

The owner of the kitten was ordered to do the clean-up. He pointed out that the clean-up should be done by the person who had smuggled it into the study. That person then pointed out the person who had fed it unsuitable mince which had caused the diarrhoea should clean up the mess. The accused person then said that the person who was bouncing the kitten until it had diarrhoea should clean up the mess.

Several days later, my son said the problem was fixed.

'By whom?' I asked.

'We had a game of poker and the loser cleaned up.'

'A perfectly logical, intelligent and fair solution,' I agreed faintly.

How To Diet

'I'm going on a diet,' my daughter announced as she came in from school.

She drifted over to the fruit bowl, peeled a banana and ate it. After she put the banana skin in the pedal bin, she cut a slice of the freshly made cheesecake.

'I have an awful figure,' she complained through her first mouthful.

I remained silent and removed the cheesecake from temptation.

'Is milk fattening?' She drifted closer to the refrigerator and opened the door to peer in. She poured out a large glass of milk and stirred in the chocolate flavouring with a heavy hand.

'Anyhow, to start my diet, I'm not having any dinner.'

'Nothing at all?'

'Well, perhaps I'll have a bowl of soup.'

I handed over the bread with the soup. She buttered three slices.

'Other people don't have to give up eating. Why have I got such a lousy figure?'

'It looks quite normal to me.'

The dedicated martyr to starvation watched as I dished up for the family, only one plate short.

'Perhaps I could have a small plate of dinner in front of telly. I do love chicken and pineapple.'

'Is it less fattening in front of telly?'

She didn't bother to answer and piled her plate high.

'I don't suppose you want any chocolate pudding for dessert?' I asked a bit later, removing the scraped-clean plate.

'Just a small helping.' An aggrieved note came into her voice. 'Remember I'm on a diet, Mum.'

She ate a small helping of chocolate pudding. There was a thoughtful silence as she noted how much was still left in the bowl. She absently finished the remainder.

'What about a hand with the dishes?'

This request triggered instant resentment.

'Gee, Mum! Why do I have to help when I'm not eating around the place? I'm not the one dirtying all the dishes!'

The Jeans Problem

'Time to get up.'

A pair of hostile eyes watched me from under the doona. 'I've got nothing to wear.'

I looked at the open drawer. A pair of clean jeans was draped across it. I picked them up and threw them on the bed.

'I can't wear those.' Out came the grievance. 'You patched them.'

'They were raggy.'

'They're ruined! Just look at them! You're always wrecking my best jeans. Nobody asked you to patch them.'

'I always patch raggy jeans.' I took a firm line. 'Otherwise they have to go into the ragbag.'

He slid further under the doona. 'Well, put them in the ragbag. I'm not wearing them.'

This was something new. I looked at the patches, neat professional and on the outside. I had been patching jeans like this for eons without complaint.

'Nobody at school wears jeans with patches.'

'There's always a first time.'

'I'll get into trouble.'

'I'll give you a note.' Notes were a great help to smooth down with the powers-that-be.

'No.'

'Wear yesterday's jeans.'

'I can't!' He really sounded upset. 'I was sliding down the grassy banks all day and they smell.'

'These are the only clean pair of jeans you have, so you'd better wear them.'

There was a pause. 'Well, go and buy me a new pair.'

'The shops aren't open.'

There was another silence. He sat up and inspected the jeans again. 'Why can't you just put little patches on them?'

'Because it takes a great big patch to cover a great big hole.'

'But everybody can see them.'

'That's the idea. Your big brother has patches on his jeans and your sisters have patches on their jeans – everybody else likes patches they can see.'

'But they have pretty patches. Mine are just plain.'

'True,' I agreed.

The others were going through a stage where patterned colourful patches were the in thing.

He pulled up his doona and burrowed down with one eye on me. 'Anyway, I'm not going to school. I haven't got anything to wear.'

'Mummy will get put in jail if you don't go to school. All children have to go to school.'

He sat up in horror. 'I thought we lived in a free country. That's not being free!'

I decided not to get involved. 'Here are your grey school shorts. You can wear them instead.'

He paled. 'Wear my school shorts! What would all my friends say?'

'I saw a lot of the boys in their school shorts.'

'Not my friends. We never wear school shorts. Only the sissies wear school shorts.'

I changed the subject. 'Aren't they your friends walking to school?'

He shot out of bed to look out the window. 'Hurry up and get my breakfast, Mum, or I'll be late.'

Five minutes later, he swaggered out, tightening the belt on his patched jeans.

Another day had begun.

Hope is Not a Method

As usual, the teenage views on life were getting beyond me. A daughter and her teenage friends had started wearing badges on their clothes with the words, 'Hope is not a method'.

'So what do all the badges mean?'

'Really, Mum! What planet are you on? The guys keep assuring us that they hope their methods will be safe.'

'Methods,' I echoed faintly as it suddenly sunk in. 'I hope you're not…'

'With those geeks and nerds? Hardly,' was the unsatisfactory reply.

The announcement that tobacco and strong drink were much more dangerous than the particular mind-altering drugs they intended to experiment with was the next shock. I didn't relax until I found the hidden pot plant with its struggling green fronds.

I helpfully watered it with boiling water every morning until the plant was discouraged enough to stay dead. This did worry the hopeful gardeners about their black thumbs but only until a new craze took over.

I just wished that all the problems raising their ugly heads in my life could be so easily managed.

Homework For Parents

I was thunderstruck! Betty Bloomer was darning! Not even socks, just a straight piece of green worsted!

Everyone in the street knew that Betty Bloomer threw holey socks away, and her children got through life with a supply of safety pins holding their clothes together.

Wendy Wooley sat beside her, tongue out in concentration, actually knitting. Wendy Wooley's girls didn't own anything hand-knitted between them, because she never knitted.

'What's up?' I asked.

Betty Bloomer looked harassed. 'It's the exams. Penny got C minus for her sewing last term. She said I had to help her. She has to hand up her darning tomorrow.'

I was silenced. Exams are very hard on parents.

Wendy Wooley didn't raise her head. 'Knit two and wool over needle,' she muttered.

'You've made good progress,' I praised.

'So I should,' she said bitterly. 'I sat up until three this morning. It's got to be handed in tomorrow. My Glenda said she'll commit suicide if she flunks her sewing again this term.'

I took that with a grain of salt. Everybody knew that Glenda was prone to dramatics.

'Wish my children were still at that stage,' I sighed wistfully. 'I want to borrow an encyclopaedia. I've got to help with an essay on whales.'

'How did you get on with your prehistoric monster for art?' Betty asked.

'B minus,' I returned savagely. 'And my son warns that he's never going to get me to help him with his art projects again.'

It still stung. I had worked all night helping finish the wretched thing and it was a very realistic monster that was carried to so proudly to school the next day.

'Half your luck,' Wendy Wooley said. 'Anyway, I heard that art teacher is very lousy with his marks.'

Betty looked up from her painstaking darning. 'Did you hear that Mrs Oddbody got marked 83% for her essay on spring?'

'She would,' I ground out. 'She pays one of those tutors to do them.'

Mrs Oddbody's daughters attended the high school in the next suburb and she was always bragging about the high marks she got.

'Anyhow, I've got to do some research.' I tucked the encyclopaedia under my arm and left.

It took me several hours to collect the information required for the essay. By the time I looked up the culture of New Guinea headhunters, heard French verbs and checked the shape and size of the latest jumbo jet, the evening was practically gone.

It was midnight before I staggered off to bed with facts and figures about whales whirling around in my mind.

I was furious when the essay was marked at only C plus. The marking system was so unfair. I had worked so hard on that essay.

Betty Bloomer was jubilant. 'Did you hear?' she babbled. 'I got A plus for my darning. Linda is so thrilled! First A she's ever got.'

Wendy was gloomy as she commiserated with me. 'I got a C minus. That teacher had the cheek to say the knitting was very uneven.' She suddenly burst into tears. 'I hate exams!'

The exam system is very hard on us parents.

The Guinea Pig Business

Some anonymous benefactor had donated a cage and four guinea pigs to the household. This was sufficient inducement for my daughter, an up-and-coming enthusiastic young businesswoman.

'Starting with three pregnant females and one male,' she calculated, 'by this time next year I should be making three dollars a week selling the surplus to the pet shop.'

Guinea pigs look like multicoloured tennis balls with tufts of fur at each end, and possess an uncanny knack of flattening themselves and squeezing through the smallest of holes in their cage to go exploring.

Unfortunately, they are not designed to cope with normal backyard perils like cats, dogs and small children. They were chased incessantly by the swarms of small children guarding them. Even the dog and the cat forgot their differences long enough to join in enthusiastic pursuit. The dog, a fat and good-natured boxer, tried hard to be helpful as he also chased wildly round and round the cage after them.

An afternoon without supervision was long enough for the first tragedy to occur. We returned home to two pathetic bodies on the front lawn and the dog ecstatically hurling them skywards under the delusion they really were tennis balls.

One of the survivors, tooting hysterically like a steam kettle, crouched under a daisy bush, while the other one was in the cage. The two bodies were buried without ceremony.

The next fatality occurred that night when the hysterical guinea pig, tooting mournfully, died in childbirth. It was buried next to its comrades.

It was a great consolation when the remaining guinea pig produced

three babies, by which time the would-be businesswoman had saved enough out walking to school instead of using the bus to invest in a fresh sire for the three babies and their mother.

A large crate was set up and made secure against escapees at the end of the yard. This was a very satisfactory arrangement until the first frost, when the entire five succumbed to exposure.

'It's not fair,' their owner mourned. 'My poor Mopsy, all my babies and my Tottles.'

And she wept bitterly as they were drummed impressively to their mass grave down an aisle of small children standing rigidly at the salute, military funerals being popular that week.

It took another month to save enough on bus fares by walking to and from school to buy a new male and a wife for him. They were duly named and entered in a fresh page of the official guinea pig stud book.

Perhaps they might have survived, producing dutifully and regularly, if their owner hadn't accepted the enticing offer of a holiday.

After a certain amount of hard-headed negotiating, her sister offered to look after them for five cents per day. She immediately scrubbed out the cage with hot water and disinfectant and ruthlessly burnt all the bedding and litter in the cage.

She did a magnificent job of keeping the cages clean and for the four agreed days they were spotless. Not a germ could have survived. Unfortunately, neither could the guinea pigs, as she refused to dirty the nice clean cage with food or bedding.

There was a certain amount of unpleasantness when the owner returned and discovered all the fatalities. More unpleasantness came when she refused to pay the carer.

'I did my job and kept them spotlessly clean,' snarled the carer.

'And they died of starvation because you refused to feed them,' screamed the bereft owner.

'At least they didn't die of disease from a filthy cage,' retorted the carer.

However, following the purchase of a new male and six females, the guinea pig breeding became more successful. In a very short space of time, the cage was wall to wall guinea pigs.

'And now,' I said thankfully, looking at the cage full of wall to wall guinea pigs. 'You can get a return on your investment and start selling two of your guinea pigs a week to the pet shop.'

The successful guinea pig breeder stared at me in horror. 'Sell my guinea pigs?' she echoed. 'After all the trouble I had raising them! I couldn't bear to part with a single one.'

'Not a single one?' I quavered, hoping I was having trouble with my hearing.

'Not a single one!' she repeated firmly.

And she didn't!

School Sick Days

It was exactly thirty minutes to countdown for the school bus and like the night before Christmas, nothing was stirring in the girls' bedroom.

'I'm dying,' came the muffled groan from under the doona. 'My stomach!'

I went across to the other bed.

'My tummy aches.'

'You've got nice rosy cheeks.'

'That's fever. Oooh, my stomach!'

I stared at the original sufferer. One bright eye watched me from behind a tangle of hair and bedclothes.

'Everybody out,' I said, feeling like a union official.

The litany of complaints was repeated.

I was unimpressed. 'The bus leaves in twenty minutes – up.'

Both mounds of bedclothes remained still. I took in orange juice, porridge and tea. Everything was downed with healthy appetites.

There was now a ten-minute countdown to the school bus.

'Everybody out,' I tried again.

'Feel my stomach – it hurts so much. You must be able to feel it?'

I obliged. All I could feel was a stomach. How did you feel somebody else's stomach ache anyway? I wasn't psychic.

'You both need a good dose of castor oil.'

One tousled head came from beneath the doona. 'What's castor oil?'

I sighed. A generation without the dread of castor oil. Just what is left to frighten the young with?

'No youth club meeting,' I threatened. 'People who aren't well enough to go to school can't go to youth club meetings.'

The malingerers were silent, digesting this threat. In the silence, the noise the bus made rumbling up the hill and past the bus stop was heard quite distinctly.

The atmosphere relaxed. Out came the knitting, the storybooks and the puzzles.

'We'll be much better by this evening,' they assured each other. 'These stomach things never last all day.'

Defeated, I retired back to my kitchen.

Two hours later, one little girl was sick. A little later, her sister copied her.

'That feels better,' she gasped. 'I feel so relieved.'

'Yes, darling,' I soothed as I washed her face. 'It is a lot better to bring it all up. You'll feel much better now.'

'It's not that. I just know you don't believe us until we have actually been sick.'

I managed to keep a straight face. 'Now where would you get an idea like that?' I asked.

What to Wear

I dutifully admired the gilt-edged invitation. It 'requested the pleasure of the fourth form girls to the fourth form boys' social.

After the first fine flush of rapture, there was a gloomy silence.

'I've got nothing to wear.' Cinderella in her cinders couldn't have sounded more tragic.

'Wear your maxi or your mini.'

'I wouldn't be seen dead in my maxi or my mini. Everybody would recognise them.'

'Your wardrobe is crammed to bursting point. There must be something you could wear.' I decided to humour this crisis. After all, clothes are important.

There was the rattle of wardrobe doors being flung wide on the mission of exploration.

'There's not a thing to wear in the house.' The heartfelt wail came from my bedroom.

I went in to investigate. All my clothes had been flung on the bed and were being subjected to critical and disdainful scrutiny.

'You're looking in the wrong wardrobe.'

A black velvet evening skirt, tight and clinging, was held up hopefully.

'No!'

A fur stole was caressed and modelled. 'I could wear it with my jeans. Then no one will notice how raggy they are.'

I shut my eyes and shuddered. The combination was exquisitely painful.

She flung herself across the bed in despair. 'My life is ruined! I just can't go!'

'What about if we make a long skirt?' I didn't want a promising life ruined at sixteen.

She sat up briskly. 'Have you got anything we can use?'

I steered her away from my remaining clothes. The only length of material suitable in the sewing box was blue taffeta.

'Yuck – nobody, but nobody wears that sort of stuff to dances!'

I heaved a sigh for the good old days when dances meant taffetas, laces and tulles. 'What are the other girls wearing?'

'Jeans, only good jeans, not raggy old ones.'

The discontent at my stinginess in not buying new jeans for the social hung in the air.

After a wearing time of discussing the pros and cons of suitable social wear, the conversation started to reach a hysterical pitch, and I was the one becoming hysterical.

I rattled my saucepans to indicate the conference was over. 'Well, if there's nothing around for you to wear, perhaps you'd better stay home after all.'

There was a long silence, punctuated only by the thoughtful sound of wardrobe doors being opened again.

'I'll wear my culottes,' came the martyred announcement. 'At least no one has seen them before.'

This great sacrifice overwhelmed me. For the sake of peaceful coexistence, I refrained from pointing out they were much too tight.

Over tea and toast the morning after the great event, she was gracious and communicative. 'Had a fab time. All the boys danced with me.'

'Well, it is nice to be popular.'

'Yeah, they had teachers hanging around and every boy who didn't get up and dance was given a detention.'

'I didn't know you'd learned how to dance. Were all your girlfriends teaching you?' I prompted, pouring out another cup of tea.

'It's easy. The band goes thump, thump, thump, and you just stand and stamp time with your feet.'

Shades of Fred Astaire! I decided to let that pass.

'What did the other girls wear?

An uninterested shrug. 'Oh, just what they wore last time. Can I have another piece of toast?'

Clean Socks For School

The clock was spinning around to countdown.

'Why aren't your shoes on?'

'I've got to dry my socks.'

'Wear another pair.'

'They've got holes in them.'

'Why are your socks wet?'

'I left them on the floor in the bathroom.'

That figured! After the morning rush of showers, there was sufficient water splashed and spilt to breed tadpoles in.

'Wear pantyhose.'

'Mum, we've got to wear socks with our summer uniform.'

'You own more than one pair of socks. What's wrong with this pair?'

'They're dirty.'

'The last wash didn't get the stains out but they are clean and dry.'

A scornful glance and she resumed her task, patiently rotating each sock over the heater.

I looked at the clock and returned to the drawer. I came out with a packaged pair, resplendent in their whiteness. 'Here's a brand-new pair.'

'I'm not wearing those!' The tone of the voice was horrified.

I suddenly felt with renewed force the communication and generation gap. 'Why not?'

The still-damp, dirty white socks were being eased carefully over feet blue with cold.

'Really, Mum! You know I like to keep one new pair aside for emergencies.'

'Isn't this an emergency?'

In the background I heard the labouring of the school bus as it wheezed up the hill.

'You just don't understand. Someday I might need those new socks.' She picked up her schoolbag and the door banged behind her.

I put the new socks back in the drawer to await the mysterious emergency and poured myself a strong cup of tea.

One of these days I was going to understand the logic of my children, but today wasn't one of them.

Mother's Day

I gazed with distaste at the cocktail sausages. The three of them, lukewarm, greasy and drowning in a pool of tomato sauce, gazed back.

'I thought we were sleeping in,' I complained. 'It is Sunday.'

'Of course,' assured my oldest daughter.

'But it's only six o'clock!'

'I wanted to be first up, so I could give you breakfast in bed.'

I forced myself to be appreciative of my greasy sausages. It is not every morning I get breakfast in bed.

'Are they nice?' she asked.

'Delicious.' I hoped I sounded convincing.

There was a terrible racket in the kitchen, the crash of crockery being broken and loud accusations and counter-accusations. I cringed down in bed. It sounded like the start of Third World War or even the end of the world.

Another daughter banged into the room. 'Mum, that little pig spilt your tea when he threw the cup at me!'

My youngest son erupted into the room, hair on end and pyjamas flapping. 'It was so my turn to bring in your cup of tea.'

'And what are you doing up?' I snarled. 'It's not a school day.'

'I know. That's why I'm up.' He was indignant. 'I don't want to waste time on a holiday.'

My greasy plate was removed. There was silence for a while and I drowsed.

I sat up as a procession entered the room. First, my oldest daughter bearing a cup half full of warm tea. Then my son behind her, carrying a saucer with two slices of lemon sloshing around in a pool of tea. My other daughter bore a bread and butter plate with one lonely jam biscuit on it.

The cup was lowered on to the saucer and given to me. They gathered around and watched like hawks. I consumed every drop of my tea and every crumb of my biscuit.

'And I brought in the lemon for your tea. That's most important,' my son told me.

'Now you can sleep in and we can get ourselves ready for church,' my younger daughter ordered.

Everyone filed out. I huddled down in bed and waited.

'Where are my socks, Mum?'

'In your drawer.'

'No, they're not.'

I rose and padded out of the bedroom, down the hall and into the other room. I opened up the drawer. Three pairs of clean white socks gazed blandly up.

'Sorry, Mum. I didn't notice them.'

'Where are all the hairbrushes?'

'In the bathroom.'

'No, they're not.'

There was one on the refrigerator, one in the fruit bowl and one in a school bag. I gathered them up without comment, put them in the bathroom and returned to bed.

My son came in. 'I cleaned my shoes.'

'They look nice and shiny,' I admired.

'Yeah, I polished them.'

He lifted his arms to hug me, displaying two black patches from wrist to elbow, standing out in bold contrast against the yellow of his windcheater.

'Why is your windcheater dirty?'

''Cause I cleaned my shoes.' He inspected his shoes proudly. 'You didn't expect me to go to church in dirty shoes.'

'Bye, Mum,' chorused his sisters. 'Enjoy your sleep-in.'

It was now seven-thirty. As soon as the door banged behind them, I crept guiltily out of bed.

Breakfast in bed is a nice thought, but I'm glad Mother's Day only comes once a year.

Low Finance

The conversation, like my finances, was getting beyond me. 'Do you mean to tell me you've lost fifty dollars?'

'Must've pulled it out with my hankie, but I won the Squash Club raffle – a bottle of pink champagne.'

'You can't layby new school shoes with a bottle of champagne.'

'I didn't see any I liked anyway.'

'So you didn't have your bus fare home then.'

'So I saved you my bus fare.' She rubbed at her heels. 'A good four-mile walk to save you the fare.'

'It's going to cost twenty dollars to have your old school shoes resoled,' I said. I took out my last twenty-dollar note. 'Get them mended on the way home from school.'

The next evening, I tried counting to ten slowly as I looked at the shabby school shoes.

'Why didn't you have them done?'

'Stand in public in my stockinged feet! What do you think I am? Everybody would have seen me.'

'Tomorrow,' I snarled.

'Well.' She smoothed out my twenty-dollar note, not looking at me. 'I've got to have ten dollars for the school dance Saturday and there's the school outing on Friday, which is eleven dollars. If you give me another dollar, we're square.'

'What about your shoes? You can't wear them like that the whole term.'

'Who cares? They're not that bad.'

There was a pause. I waited suspiciously.

'What about a new dress?'

'You've just got a new dress.'

'Unsuitable.'

'The velveteen?'

'Too hot.'

'Your new red jersey?'

'Not for the school dance.'

The conversation lapsed. The thoughtful silence built up. I waited.

'I saw this dress.'

'I haven't got any money.'

'Only fifty dollars and what about my student allowance? Isn't it supposed to clothe me?'

'School shoes,' I struggled.

'It's a voile, middy with a ruffled hem. It fitted me so perfectly I asked them to put it aside until I could collect it. Please, Mum. This is important.'

I fought a losing rearguard battle. 'You need some decent underwear.'

'Nobody wears underwear, Mum. This is an emergency. I can't go to the school dance in rags. What sort of example will I set?'

I gave up the unequal struggle.

I wondered about that example too.

The Viking Funeral

'Mum!' someone screamed. 'My electric blanket isn't working!'

The winter brings quite a few problems around our house apart from coughs and colds. Lives fall under the baleful influence of electric blankets. One school of thought believes that if switching them on an hour before going to bed warms the sheets, leaving them on full blast all day ensures a much warmer bed.

During economy campaigns, I stormed around the bedrooms during the day switching them off. I followed closely all the news items about house fires inexplicably started, burning the occupants to death.

'Electric blankets left on all day,' I reported.

My children of the technological age are unconvinced.

'They've got automatic controls, Mum – don't panic.'

During tribal warfare, it was a favourite tactic to pull out each other's plugs. This left the enemy really in the cold at bedtime.

One of the addicts had been having trouble with her control. The smell of burning and the haze of blue smoke proved to be a burnt-out switch, impressive enough to have burnt a hole in the sheet and scorched the mattress.

I took it off the bed. The addict was desolate – and cold. She bribed her small brother to change beds for the week. Ten cents and half her chocolates, spoils from the latest admirer.

'Tut!' said the man of the house as he shortened the cord to find new wires. 'Nearly at the end of its tether.'

The blanket lasted another few weeks and blew up with a dramatic 'phut'.

'Another hole in the sheet,' reported the addict.

I stripped the bed, and listened to the negotiations.

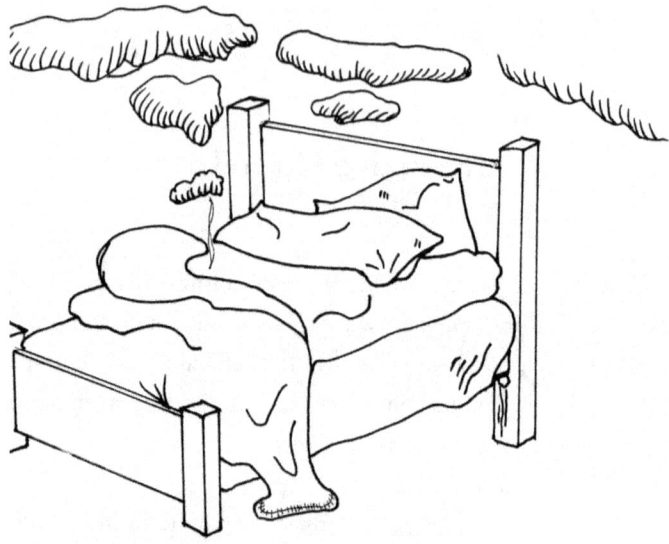

'But I haven't got any more chocolates!'

'What about your honey crunches?'

'I need them to sustain me.'

'Please yourself,' said the occupant of the warmest bed in the house with a most Gallic shrug. 'I won't swap.'

It was a cold night so the addict took a last wistful look at her packet of honey crunch and handed over.

'Damn kids,' grumbled the man of the house. 'They must swing on the controls to wreck them like this.'

It was a freezing cold morning when the plug went again. I watched the smoke curling up.

'Do you want to be incinerated? Get out of that bed!'

'Like a Viking funeral,' said the addict, laying there and watching the blue haze wreathe up around her. 'So romantic!'

'That's the end!' I pulled the addict out, took the blanket off the bed and headed out to the rubbish bin.

Behind me, I heard the persuasive tones of the addict.

'Wake up, sleepy. 'I'll swap you some chewing gum and my best black biro for your bed.'

As I say, winter brings its problems!

The Lost Football

My son arrived home for lunch carrying a football. He patted it admiringly. 'I found it.'

'Who lost it?' I queried.

He took another mouthful of bread and jam. 'It's harder than mine and nearly new.'

'What about handing it in?'

He considered for a moment and took another bite of his bread and jam. 'My ball is old and soft. This one is a lot better.'

'But it isn't yours.'

There was an awkward pause.

'I'll put it away carefully,' he said and vanished into his bedroom.

He returned and continued eating bread and jam.

I tried to appeal to his better instincts. 'Some poor little boy is going to go home to his mummy and tell her he's lost his new football.'

'It's not brand-new, it's all used. If you tried to sell it, it would only be worth about twenty cents, I bet.'

'You wouldn't like a little boy to pick up your football and take it home and put it in his wardrobe…'

Large brown eyes stared thoughtfully into mine as he contemplated the dreadful thought. 'I look after my football. I don't leave it in the middle of a bush.'

'Take it back to school and give it to the headmaster.'

'The headmaster's not on yard duty and we aren't allowed inside.'

'Give it to the teacher on yard duty.'

He shuffled his feet. 'I can't do that. They have different teachers looking after different grades. I'm not allowed in the other part of the schoolyard.'

I sighed.

He capitulated. 'I'll go and ask in all the classrooms.'

'You won't be allowed,' I pointed out. 'Take the football back to school and give it to your teacher.'

'She's not interested in football.'

I sighed again. He went back into the bedroom and came out with the football, giving it a trial toss in the air.

'Probably belongs to a prep and they're too little to play football. I'll mind it.'

Something snapped. 'Take it back and hand it up or I will.'

'But it's lost, Mum. Don't you understand? I found it over the school fence. It doesn't belong to anybody.'

I put my cup down with a slam.

'All right. I'm going.'

I stood at the gate and watched. The football got dribbled down the lane with magnificent hand passes past the rubbish bins; was punted over the main road into the school ground and promptly vanished under a yelling crowd of small boys.

I went back inside. I always find the school lunch break very tiring.

Lost and Found

The house and yard were deserted. There was no sight or sound of any children around. The peace and quiet made me uneasy. They had all gone blackberrying and promised they wouldn't go too far. I went hunting.

Half an hour up a back road, I came across a procession.

First, came one little boy, wobbling all over the road on a bike too big for him. An unknown boy wobbled along on another bike behind him with three empty billycans threaded across the handles. Then came the dog behind them. The permanently worried look on his face looked deeper than usual.

Two dusty little girls dragged between them by ropes and chains their captive. It was a large and reluctant goat, all long horns and whiskers. I studied it doubtfully.

'Isn't it beautiful,' said one daughter.

'No! Where did you get it?'

'It was lost and we found it.'

'Can we keep it, and what sex do you reckon it is?' asked my practical daughter.

I peered at it. With all that long hair, it was hard to work out. The goat glared at me, lowered its head and charged in my direction.

The dog shot behind me looking worried. You could see he didn't approve of goats.

'Isn't it playful?' one daughter said fondly, choking off the goat's sudden rush.

'Looks unfriendly,' I remarked, moving further away.

'Can we keep it, please?'

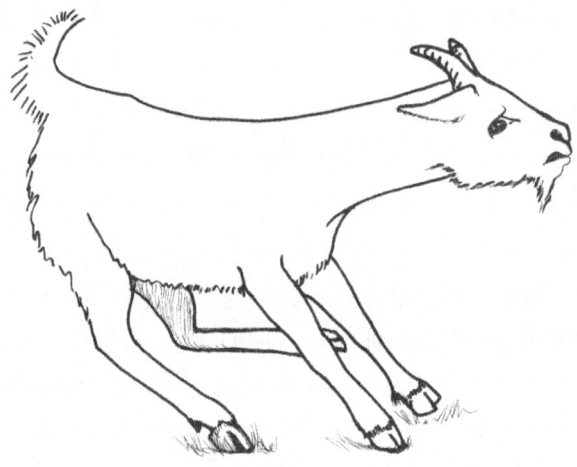

'You have,' I intoned, chanting a litany, 'six guinea pigs, one budgie, one rabbit, two mice, one dog, one cat and one horse.'

'We thought we could mind it until we found its owner,' my daughter explained, turning her usual deaf ear to my litany.

'Yeah, and put an ad in the paper about it being lost.'

'Go to the pet shop and get them to put a notice in their window.'

There was a thoughtful silence.

'Someone might see it,' mused one small boy.

'That's the idea,' I snapped.

We reached home. The goat was tied to a tree with the dog's water bucket in easy reach and a pile of fresh lawn clippings. The children sat around in admiration.

'You'd better go down to the pet shop and get them to put a notice in the window,' I nagged.

'We will later.'

'Yeah, maybe tomorrow.'

'Will I have to go over to the pet shop to put the notice in?' I asked.

The threat worked. There were a chorus of aggrieved protests. The hopeful owners of the lost goat headed slowly down the road towards the pet shop.

Later, they all came back, still with the aura of injury around them.

'If no one claims it, can we have it?'

'It'll get claimed,' I promised with far more confidence than I was feeling.

'It was a very small notice. Perhaps the owner won't notice it.'

'I've always wanted a goat,' one daughter sighed.

'No.'

The children stared reproachfully at me, united by their bewilderment at my totally unreasonable attitude.

'Don't be dishonest! The goat belongs to someone and goats cost money,' I said defensively.

'How much money?' My son had ticker tapes of calculation flicking behind his brown eyes.

I was lost! I couldn't remember where I had ever seen the going price of a goat, sex unknown. 'Lots of money.'

'How much?'

'Seventy-five dollars,' I guessed wildly.

There was an impressed silence.

'Well, at least we've got him until tomorrow.'

'Maybe all this week,' said the optimist of the family.

'Maybe it'll like us so much, it'll stay for good,' someone else said.

'Go wash your hands,' I ordered sternly, wondering why my family made me feel so tired all the time. 'Dinner's ready.'

Harmony

The picnic lunch was supposed to be an exercise in cooperation.

'Why don't you get cracking on the wood?'

'What happened to the water?'

'Can't heat a billy without fire.'

'Well, I'm not feeding your fire. I'll start my own.'

'I'm not going down the creek for water to boil in your billy – get your own.'

'It's my billy, anyway.'

'All right, selfish. So stick it on your own fire.'

'I will – and I won't share.'

Peace descended, and into the air rose the smoke of three fires tended by three uncooperative little savages.

The Good Samaritan

The Good Samaritan was driving along a country road when she spotted the two rottweilers bounding along. Everyone knows that it is dangerous and illegal for dogs to be running free without their owners around.

She got out of the car. The two rottweilers snarled in a very threatening manner. She got back into the car and tried herding them from the car on to the footpath. This actually worked.

At last, one of them headed down a driveway. Ah! They knew the way home.

She drove into the driveway, unbolted the heavy gate to the back yard and the two dogs bounded in. She rebolted the gate and with a virtuous heart knocked on the front door.

A lady opened it.

Did she own rottweilers?

Yes, she had two.

The Good Samaritan explained she had just returned them. There were mutual exchanges of gratitude and modest no problems and the Good Samaritan left.

She noticed as she backed her car out of the driveway that two rottweilers were snarling at her through one of the front windows. So unhygienic to have such large animals in the house.

She also noticed an extra two rottweilers snarling at her through the bars of the heavy gate to the backyard.

Feeling it was unnecessary to further complicate her life, she drove off.

Life in the Seventies

Women's liberation arrived with Germaine Greer. The Sputnik and the Beatles arrived. Fast food entrenched itself. Children adopted the custom of eating out with enthusiasm and the years of the three basic takeaways – meat pies, saveloys and fish and chips – became a historical joke.

Teenage sons blossomed into confident and exotic youths with shoulder-length hair, see-through floral blouses, flared pants and gold chains around their necks for special parties. Houses reverberated to the pounding beat of rock music and shrieked songs without lyrics.

They moved into flower power, acceptance of topless bathing and the Age of Aquarius. They were contemptuous of the material and worldly ideology of their elders. Tobacco and strong drink were much more dangerous than the particular mind-altering drugs they experimented with. Their respective fathers were not amused.

The battle over hair lengths raged for years and years. Despite the fortune used in the daily use of shampoos and conditioners, any hair longer than the ears was considered dirty and disgusting. Long hair led to immorality and subversive attitudes to society and every male over forty agreed wholeheartedly.

Mealtimes, the only domestic timetable that teenage youths attended with religious punctuality, became battle zones. The heads of households fought every inch of the way. They sneered, jeered, mocked, yelled and worried endlessly about the new generation. They had raised sons to be poofters and effeminate layabouts and simultaneously, depraved immoral sex perverts whom they accused spent their time having orgies.

In turn, superior scorn and contempt were poured on their father's academic background.

'Really, Dad, what would you know? The atom wasn't even split when you were at school.'

The heads of households kept up their similar litanies endlessly, day after day and month after month. Sons' only hobbies were taking drugs, wasting money on personal adornment and marching endlessly to protest against everything their careful elders had set in place, ignoring the advantages of their expensive educations and the benefits of studying towards socially acceptable jobs.

Raised on the heroic myths of the Australian legend, fathers were shocked and disbelieving at unpatriotic, disloyal sons who marched against conscription and the Vietnam War and burned draft cards.

I was shocked at being expected to participate in all the new ideology.

'Take the day off work to march carrying a placard?' I gasped.

I never found out what they were protesting about, but it was right on stocktaking and we were frantically busy.

It was so hard to be supportive of the new ideologies when you worked.

Gifts for the Grateful

It was the best-seller of all best-sellers, slightly feminist, witty and so funny. I acquired it three weeks before my daughter's birthday. I had finished reading it and was contemplating wrapping it in suitable birthday paper when my other daughter strolled in.

'You got a copy,' she gasped. 'I've just got to read it.'

'It's a birthday present.'

'Her birthday is a good three weeks away. I'm a speed reader. You can have it back tomorrow.'

Three days later, it was still missing. 'My neighbour said she'd finish it overnight,' my daughter admitted.

One week later, it was still missing.

'Well, Jilly's cousin took it with her when she went away for the weekend.'

Two weeks later, it was still missing.

'Where is it?' I demanded.

'She gave it back to my neighbour, who then lent it to her sister, who lent it to her daughter, who lent it to her girlfriend who lent it to –'

I tried not to sound hysterical. 'Your large neighbourhood of best friends can borrow it from the library, not use my birthday copy. Either that book is returned or I will charge you all lending fees – very high ones.'

The night before my daughter's birthday, the book arrived back for wrapping. It didn't look brand-new any more. The cover was ripped. The brown patches on some of the pages looked like either tea or coffee stains. Some smoker had burned holes in some of the more exciting descriptions. Most of the pages had dog-eared corners where they had been turned down.

'Why am I getting a second-hand book for my birthday?' the birthday girl demanded in a very ungrateful tone as she unwrapped her present.

'It's the latest and most popular best-seller,' I said weakly.

And she didn't even thank me for it.

Transport

My oldest son got his driving licence. I suddenly was a pedestrian. He spent his time running members of entire football teams and school socials to and fro with the family car, a beetle-shaped Volkswagen.

There were the usual screaming fits by his father on the mornings after the car was borrowed.

'How can you get five hundred miles up on the speedo when you only had to drive one mile down the road to your school social last night?'

'Gee, Dad. I had to pick up all the girls, and some lived in Croydon and some lived in Tullamarine and some lived out past –'

'Forget it!' His father suddenly got even more unreasonable about the demands on his purse and his car. 'How come I have to pay out for him to take some bird somewhere that I certainly can't afford to go? And I can't afford to go anywhere because I have to pay out for his social life.'

Then the even more unworthy suspicions surfaced after his son had organised a party for the visiting football team. The entire car from glovebox to back seating area and the space under the front bonnet was carefully searched before the car and its passengers were allowed to head off to yet another party.

'Gee, Dad,' howled his exasperated son. 'What do you think I have hidden in the car, a double bed?'

I wasn't sure if his father really was searching for a double bed in the Volkswagen beetle, but it did shut up him – until the next time.

High Finance

A financial expert tried to inculcate in me the mysteries of economics.

'So you spend a dollar.'

'Yes.'

'The person who has your dollar also spends it. That makes two dollars spent.'

'Er – yes.'

'By the time ten people have spent that same dollar, that's ten dollars doing the rounds of the economy.'

'Um – but it's still only one dollar.'

'No, dum dum – it then becomes ten dollars to boost the economy.'

It was very confusing. However, I had an example much nastily closer to home.

My youngest son had enrolled at a tertiary institution. This was definitely a step in the right direction. He also enrolled in all the other sports, hobbies and other necessary diversions to relieve the tedium of solid study at that institution.

Suddenly, he needed $500 in a hurry. It was union fees, book money, upfront money for something needed for his degree, he confessed vaguely and a bit gloomily.

His older sister, on a lucrative wage in her high-profile profession, magnanimously donated the money, waving aside the feeble promises to repay.

'If it's going to help with getting a degree, it's for a good purpose.'

Her Good Samaritan and benevolent attitude towards her little brother lasted exactly three months. She spent some of her spare time scuba diving. A hint of a rumour reached her ears. Then there were an undignified and totally unladylike explosion, a tantrum and gangster-like threats.

'He put that money towards a scuba diving expedition up north! I can't even afford a holiday up north because I'm subsidising his pleasures. He can return my money pronto or else.'

'He was made dive master of the scuba diving club, so I suppose he had to go. And he is only a student and can't produce that sort of money out of thin air,' I protested weakly.

'I don't mind selling his body to the medical faculty, or maybe draining his blood and selling it overseas to get my money back,' his unnatural sister threatened. 'And he's never getting another cent out of me on any pretext.'

There was a lot of unease around the family for a while.

At last, a tolerant family friend advanced a loan of $500 to repay the irate debtor. Peace descended.

Except my youngest son, in the first throes of getting wheels and a driving licence, borrowed the tolerant family friend's car and returned it in less than immaculate condition.

'Hum,' said the family friend to my youngest son, inspecting the damage and suddenly a whole lot less tolerant. 'I think you had better repay my loan. I'm going to need it to pay the panel beater.'

My youngest son seemed to have a lot of calls on whatever money he collected in his part-time work and found it very difficult to put together the amount of $500. The weeks slid past. The family friend became less and less tolerant and less and less family-friendly.

The situation looked like developing into another nasty debtor/creditor situation by the time the loan was at last repaid.

'Where did you get the money?' I demanded.

'Borrowed it off my cousin.'

'But you'll have to repay it,' I wailed. 'He has less money than the rest of you.'

'Don't nag. I'll repay him.'

'When?'

'As soon as I can.'

This was unsatisfactory. I thought it was dreadful that his dumb cousin had lent him the money with no chance of ever seeing it again. I agonised often enough to upset my son on his rare visits.

'Well, you can shut up about it,' he said one day. 'I paid him back.'

'The full amount of $500?'

'Of course. Don't you think I have any principles?'

I was so thankful. It was nice to know that I had raised my youngest son to understand about principles. It took me a long time to discover that he had borrowed the money from his other sister, after swearing her to secrecy.

It was the undignified fight when he discovered that she had advertised his cross-country skis for sale because he was so slow at repaying the loan that had caused her impulsive and much-regretted generosity to come out.

'I'm going overseas and I need that money,' she demanded. 'Pay up or else.'

He was very bitter over his sister's mercenary streak and a lot of dirty linen and sundry other matters were raised before he promised to pay within the next seven days.

He promptly borrowed the money from his big brother. His eldest sister took off on her travels. Peace descended around the family.

I did keep wondering who else was left to pay back big brother and timidly raised the question as to whether big brother expected to be paid back.

'Doesn't matter,' big brother shrugged. 'His honesty and credit standing is much too important to be jeopardised by a measly $500.'

I was relieved that the need for another gullible lender for the unfortunate $500 was over, but I still wonder.

According to my financial expert, $500 doing the rounds four times meant that the economy was enriched by $2,000. I'm still not convinced. The economy can't be ready for that sort of financial boosting, not to mention the accrued acrimony rippling further and further through the society of gullible lenders. But I have to confess that economics and high finance are still beyond me.

Rolls Royce Driving

I was being told about how an ex Rolls Royce chauffeur had to drive – no sudden acceleration, no sudden braking, all very smooth in respect of that wonderful engine. I remembered wistfully I had never been behind the wheel of a Rolls Royce.

Once upon a time, I drove every car model on the road. This was because as soon as I acquired my driving licence, I was conscripted into becoming a jockey for a repossession agent.

This was back in the days when credit facilities were a generous open door for electrical goods, furniture and of course cars. Repayments were not so effortless, so the occupation of repossession agents appeared. They had to be tough and ruthless, as the chapter and verse of repossession contracts were really rough. Women fought over losing their new washing machines and men got desperate over losing their cars.

As a repossession jockey, I drove sports cars with dashboards like aeroplane cockpits; customline cars, driving like railway carriages and taking up just as much room on the road; sedans of all sorts of makes and sizes, mainly either with no brakes, no first gears and no decent steering.

This caused an instant interest in all car parts. I often drove trucks – although not interstate ones. Mostly ones covered with loose, rusty and dinted sheeting and usually no brakes – I always got a courteous right of way on crossroads whether I was in the right or the wrong.

I was again regretful that I never drove a Rolls Royce. Then again, if someone had enough finance to afford a Rolls Royce, they probably wouldn't get repossessed.

As I was a wife as well as a jockey, I never got paid for my work, but I suppose working as a jockey did improve my driving no end even without that one missing experience.

Car Matters

I paid out eleven dollars for a second-hand battery for my elderly Austin station wagon. That kept it moving the full six years I drove it. It was very reliable and went and went.

Unfortunately, it didn't stop as efficiently. It was always having brake trouble. If it wasn't brake drums, or brake shoes, it was something else! This made me a very careful driver, as I placed no reliance on the brakes at all, and coasted to a stop or used the gears to slow down.

I objected to a family member using it. He drove too fast and with a trusting faith in brakes.

It is so true that there is no harmony in a household with two driving licences and one car.

The only time it ever refused to restart was at a stop light in the pouring rain. I had reconnected the battery the wrong way around. I ordered the brawny son to get out and give me a push.

He buried his head under the back seat wailing. 'The humiliation, the humiliation of it all! What if someone sees me?'

There was all this family embarrassment. I had to accept that it was time for my Austin station wagon to go to that great parking lot in the sky.

Yoda

I was delighted to be informed at last that I was to be a grandmother.

My daughter had been the last remnant of the flower power era. She was very liberated and modern and I didn't really expect her to ever suffer from the threat of her biological clock running out.

She had come back from overseas and decided on marriage. There had been the usual problems. She wanted to wear cheesecloth and fresh flowers and be married barefoot on the surf beach. Her father, a man of conservative habits, refused to be a party to a beach wedding.

With great difficulty, we reconciled her to the idea of a church wedding, but not as a traditional bride.

She decided to be unusual and innovative in red. 'I mean, just consider how dashing a bright red veil misting up to the altar will be.'

I wasn't conservative, but I protested. There was a delicate compromise: pale blue, pearls and an unusual headdress. After that, she had decided that it was silly to become a mother too late in life, so therefore she was going to have a baby.

There seemed no problems with the pregnancy. She didn't suffer from morning sickness or any other disadvantage like excessive weight. She gave up smoking and drinking, but otherwise just ignored her pregnancy to the stage that she still wore clothes that pushed against her baby bulge alarmingly until I complained.

At seven and a half months along, I was knitting booties, as became a new grandmother, and dreaming about my very first brand-new grandchild, when she dropped her bombshell.

'I've been thinking! I've changed my mind. I don't want to have a baby.'

'You can't change your mind!'

'I can and I will. I think it's a silly idea. I mean, the world is overpopulated as it is. I'm not ready to become a mother.'

'But you can't change your mind. The baby's practically due to be born.'

'Garbage!'

I trotted her off for her prenatal check-ups. The doctor gave her a good talking to. The matron of the hospital gave her a good talking to.

I grimly kept driving her to her prenatal birthing sessions. It was a lost cause. I watched as the line of bulging would-be new mothers huffed and puffed, practising their breathing for having a baby. My daughter uncooperatively just sat, cross-legged and bulging at the end of the line, hair over her face concealing her sulky expression.

I didn't get discouraged. I drove her in every week for her check-ups and her exercise sessions. She refused to think about or discuss baby clothes, bassinets or prams. My very pregnant daughter continued to drift through life with her nose in lurid science fiction novels, ignoring her pregnancy and any forward planning associated with it. She was working on the theory that if she ignored her pregnancy for long enough, it would just go away. I started to really worry about the fate of my first grandchild.

Came an afternoon, her husband rang in a panic. He suspected she had gone into labour. She was still ignoring her pregnancy and had refused to time her pains. He tried to bundle her into hospital, timing her pains with an increasing panic. She insisted he stop at the first bookshop so she could get something to read first to alleviate the tedium and boredom of hospital.

She drifted through the bookshop browsing. Her husband timed her pains and kept ringing me. By the time she had found a book that was to her satisfaction, her pains were down to five-minute intervals.

The next call was from the hospital. The pains had stopped and she wanted to come home again. I was really feeling sorry for my son-in-law. He flatly refused to drive her home again. He sounded a quivering wreck and announced he was going to get a divorce.

There were a few hours without phone calls. I went to bed. I was woken out of a sound sleep at one a.m. to be told that the labour pains had started again. I muttered congratulations and tried to go back to sleep. I was rung back at two a.m. to be informed the pains were coming at two-minute intervals. I suggested to my son-in-law that he go in and hold his wife's hand and make positive noises.

The next phone call was at six a.m. My son-in-law sounded disbelieving. Without too much fuss and doubtless still reading her chosen science fiction novel, his wife had produced a very small son.

I decided to visit during visiting hours so she would have some time to rest. I spent most of the morning agonising and worrying. She hadn't wanted the baby and seemed very uninterested in all the drama of pregnancy and birth. What if she rejected the baby now it was born? What if she refused to feed it? What if she went into postnatal depression?

The baby slept in a bassinet beside her bed. By comparison to her husband who looked haggard and about ten years older than twenty-four hours ago, my daughter looked rested, bright-eyed and smug.

I had a cuddle of the baby and my heart sank. It was not the sort of baby to attract my daughter's admiration. It was not the sort of baby to attract anyone's admiration. It didn't even look like a human baby. It looked like some sort of weird alien.

It was unfortunate that it was a barely six-pound baby, which meant that it was wrinkled and scrawny. It also had a bald skull coming to a distinct point – something like a Klingon, or was it a Kleeon, out of *Star Trek* television episodes. It had slanting eyes, vividly bright blue (did we have any Mongolian or Chinese blood in the family, I wondered) and ears that floated out like Dumbo the elephant's and a generally bewildered, unfinished look to it. It gave me a wavery insecure sort of grin and my heart turned over.

'Very cute,' I said.

'Isn't he?' agreed my daughter. 'He looks exactly like Yoda out of *Star Wars*.'

I muttered reluctant agreement. He did look exactly like Yoda. Was it the influence of that constant diet of science fiction during the pregnancy?

The unnamed baby wrinkled his face up even more, opened his mouth and bellowed. It was a surprisingly loud bellow for such a small baby.

A nurse arrived, lifted him up and thumped him. 'Wind,' she said.

'I'll take him,' the modern liberated stranger who was my daughter said. 'He's due for another feed anyway. No need to starve him on his first day of life.'

'Glad you like him,' I said weakly.

'Exactly what I wanted,' my daughter said happily. 'I would have so hated to have had a boring dull baby exactly the same as the other dodoes in the ward.'

I tottered off home. I was a grandmother, and the pressures of the pregnancy were over at last.

'Thank God it's all over,' my son-in-law said with a sigh.

'It's not all over,' I enlightened him sympathetically. 'It's all just beginning.'

I suppose I would even get used to a name like Yoda if that was what was decided. Actually, to my relief I didn't have to. But that's another story.

The Musical Talent

The youngest grandson had started violin lessons and was taking them seriously. I was most impressed. It was so nice to have musical talent in the family.

'He intends to go busking over the Christmas holidays,' his mother explained, wincing at the discordant wails coming from the back veranda.

'And only been learning for six weeks.' I was even more impressed.

Over the holidays, all the musically talented kids littered up the shopping centre with their musical instruments, busking, open cases at their feet, all hopefully waiting for appreciative patrons to enrich them.

By the holidays, my inexpert ears hadn't noticed that the discordant wails from the violin actually played a recognisable tune, but I had to give full marks for his dedication in practising.

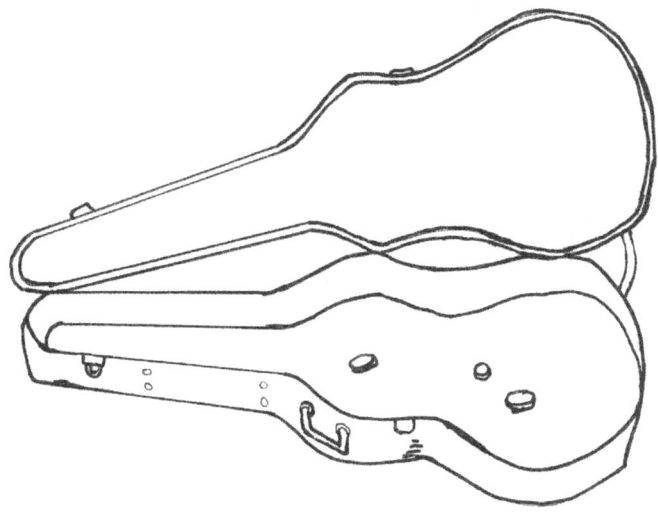

So I can't say how proud I was to see the fair-haired little eight-year-old, blue eyes scowling purposefully as he stood in front of his open case busking away beside the usual line-up of talented kids.

I dropped several coins into his case and listened to the almost recognisable wails of 'Three Blind Mice'. As it was the only tune he had mastered, he played it over and over again to the unappreciative shoppers.

After the holidays, he gave away the violin and took up the trumpet and his mother took up earmuffs.

'No money in violins,' he explained. 'Only made eighty cents busking.'

And it was my eighty cents after all.

Reading to Children

As a grandmother, I was interested in the new mother's obsession with the theory that reading to children should be started from a very young age.

The theory that fathers should be more involved in such hands-on action caused more than the usual ripples in the marriage. Voices started to rise over the demanding screams from the overtired child.

'I've got to study up for some talks I'm listed to give.'

'Your daughter's potential intelligence is of more importance than your silly lectures.'

There was muttered surrender. The defeated loser trudged off to the bedroom, picture book under on arm and baby under the other.

Then the measured cadences of the soothing male voice reading floated up the passage and peace settled.

After a while, I went to inspect. The picture book was on the floor. My granddaughter was tucked under Daddy's arm, wide blue eyes watching with unblinking attention as she listened to her favourite reader intoning carefully the listed specifications of jet engines.

I tiptoed out again. I wasn't sure how the listed specifications of jet engines could improve the potential intelligence quotient of a twelve-month-old baby girl but the house was peaceful, which was the most important thing.

The Guinea Pig Saga

The saga of the guinea pigs, like the rest of the pets in that family, was ongoing. There was always a high mortality rate. They got killed by dogs, cats or extremes of temperature, or they escaped. It was fortunate that they bred so industriously.

One morning, as often happened in the cage of wall-to-wall guinea pigs, two of them became mothers. One produced her two babies with her usual predictable regularity. The other had problems. She gave birth to a baby guinea pig and then what seemed to be most of her insides.

The four young owners gathered around and watched in disgusted awe.

'We'll have to take her to the vet's to be made better,' the particular ten-year-old owner of the unfortunate guinea pig decided.

'I happen to be busy,' my daughter apologised. 'Maybe later.'

This set off a terrible outcry. Didn't their mother care that their favourite guinea pig might die? The entreaties turned to tantrums and then tears.

Ten minutes later, the vet's crowded waiting room witnessed the arrival of one distracted mother with the sick guinea pig, being swept through to the emergency section by a wave of howling children.

The vet turned his back on his crowded waiting room to cope with this emergency. He held the guinea pig under the running tap to clean most of the dirt and mess off it, and sent the worried owners out to wait in the waiting room while he got to work.

A few minutes later, the worried owners rushed in to survey the invalid. She rested, eyes closed, spreadeagled out on a towel on top of a hot water bottle, a guinea pig-sized anaesthetic mask over her muzzle.

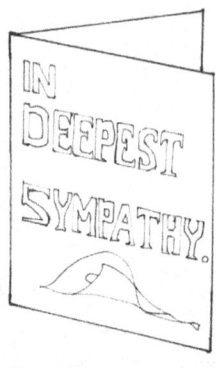 

Her pulsating insides were inside her where they belonged. The vet nurse, a most conscientious attendant sat beside her, drying her with a hairdryer.

The guinea pig mother had had a prolapse, the vet explained, and there was still another baby waiting to be born, but she might not manage it. This set off another series of wails.

The vet then assured his wailing clients that if the mother couldn't have the baby normally, he would do a Caesarean section and while he was doing it he would give the guinea pig a hysterectomy. Then he had to explain what a hysterectomy was. The four owners gave this careful thought and approved. The vet then promised to ring if there were any developments and ushered them out.

When they arrived home, they were relieved to discover that two busy guinea pig mothers were sharing the workload of raising the three babies born that morning. At least the orphan was going to survive.

I heard a day or two later that the vet had rung to report that the guinea pig and its unborn baby had not survived. This was a real domestic tragedy.

'I suppose everyone is a bit upset,' I consoled.

'Not as upset as I'm going to be about the bill,' their mother wailed.

And receiving his bill, she remained unconsoled, despite the lovely sympathy card the vet sent the four mourning owners.

I always said that vet had a lovely bedside manner.

Sherry

'It would be nice if Sherry had a baby before she got too old,' the mother of the household said one day to the family.

The pets of the household were a dog, three cats, several guinea pigs and a budgie. Sherry the Welsh mountain pony, a middle-aged placid spinster and gone to fat as the middle-aged often are, was the most favourite pet.

There were cries of delight from the four children, Sherry's most devoted fans and admirers.

'A pure silver foal,' Rose said.

'Or a bright golden one,' Noela sighed.

'Are you sure there are no such things as flying horses?' the small Jeff asked hopefully.

'It would be so nice to have a flying horse,' Mary the middle daughter agreed.

'There's a difference between reality and fairy tales,' their mother said, wondering if she should have censored their reading more carefully. 'If you study up about horse colours, you'll understand what colour her foal will be.'

This led to a rush on the book about horse colours and there were great and learned discussions about how to organise that Sherry's foal would be a palomino. This ended in Sherry being taken down to the local stud and introduced to a handsome palomino stallion.

Sherry almost swooned when he greeted her. It was love at first sight, the fans all agreed. Sherry then went to her fate with unmaidenly enthusiasm.

She spent the next eleven months in the equivalent of Welsh mountain pony paradise. She was not ridden nor worked for fear of overtiring

her. She was plied with the correct prenatal goodies to make sure her baby would be healthy.

With each drawn-out month that passed, her stomach bulged out even further. At this stage, she couldn't have been ridden anyway because no girth straps would meet around that interesting bulge. The fans and admirers patted and felt the bulge possessively, declaring they could feel baby pony bits.

After the eleventh month and the due-by date had come and gone, the disappointed watchers demanded the vet come along and *make* the new pony appear.

'Not pregnant,' the vet said to the shocked fans. 'Either the stud didn't take or something went wrong.'

'What about her fat tummy?' challenged the disappointed Rose.

'She's spent months stuffed with all those prenatal goodies and not working. Wonder she didn't founder,' sniffed the vet as she packed up and left.

The stud then offered a free service to the disappointed family. The handsome palomino stallion had died of old age or overwork, but they had another stallion on offer, not a palomino and not as good-looking of course. The disappointed admirers set up a terrible outcry. Sherry just had to have a silver or golden baby pony. There was much sulking before they grudgingly agreed to settle for an ordinary-looking baby.

Sherry was taken back down to the stud and introduced to the new stallion. She greeted him with her usual lack of modesty and much enthusiasm. This time, she stayed at the stud until the pregnancy was safely along before being returned.

The months slid past. Despite the prenatal goodies she was fed, her middle-age spread didn't spread any further. This was a continuing worry. The fans and admirers patted and probed. Perhaps she wasn't pregnant? Where was the new baby going to grow if she didn't get fat?

Against all groans about the expense, the vet had to be called to verify she was still pregnant. The vet came, confirmed that she was, soothed the admirers and left.

The due date of the happy event came and then went. This time, it was the worried mother who rang the vet.

The vet was busy and less than cooperative about being expected to drop her other work to rush over just to reassure everyone. 'If she's going to have trouble giving birth, there'll be plenty of time to let me know. If she's not going to have trouble, you won't need me,' she said crisply and hung up.

Everyone still worried.

'What if Sherry had her baby and no one knew?' Rose wailed.

'What if she was too weak to protect it from foxes or wild dogs?' Noela worried.

'What about horse rustlers?' demanded Jeff, whose television diet seemed to consist of cowboy movies.

'We don't have packs of wild dogs or horse rustlers in this area,' snapped their mother. 'And foxes don't attack horses.'

'We could sleep in her paddock to protect her,' Jeff suggested.

'Brilliant,' agreed Mary.

'Definitely not,' snapped their mother.

Sherry remained placid, uninterested in everyone unless bearing edible goodies, and still looked unpregnant. The days slid past. The vet, when rung, promised to turn up the next week if Sherry hadn't dropped her foal.

Early the morning after the call to the vet, there was a phone call from the owner of the paddock reporting that Sherry had dropped her foal. Everyone rushed over to the paddock. Sherry was grazing in her usual spot by the dam.

There was no sign of a foal! Sherry's baby, as so gloomily predicted, must have been killed and eaten by foxes, or packs of dogs! There was a gale of disappointed sighs from fans and admirers who then started their noisy mourning.

Sherry heard her admirers and trotted up to visit. What looked like a small pile of manure lifted on unsteady legs and followed her up. The cries of grief stopped and became glad outcries of pleasure.

The new member of the household was about the size and build of a skinny undersized greyhound, with neat black hooves the size of twenty-cent pieces. It had a short moth-eaten-looking mane and a dispirited raggy-looking tail. Its muzzle was narrow and sharp and its ears were the wrong shape and poking out in the wrong direction. Its body wasn't at all horse-shaped.

After the fans and admirers were reassured that the peculiar-looking thing wobbling around on four spindly short legs really would grow into a proper pony, they moved in to inspect and examine.

The foal was nervous at first, but a few minutes later allowed herself to be patted and touched. With each pat and touch, the fans and admirers became less critical and more wholehearted in their admiration and devotion. She was so cute and she reciprocated their curiosity and love at first sight. None of them minded that she didn't even look like a pony.

Sherry took all the praise about her cleverness as placidly as usual and then headed back to her usual grazing spot, her daughter following as if attached by an invisible string.

There was a barrage of satisfied sighs as she left. And there was not one single complaint that the new pony was the same colour as the manure in the paddock and not a dashing silver or gold as had been demanded.

Having a Family

Having a family is…

Someone to cut the lawns that never grow because of the traffic.

White mice breeding with house mice and a cat too well fed to catch either of them.

Someone breeding rabbits the same time as someone brings home their first ferret.

Serving your guests cooking sherry because the good sherry has been used up on sick animals.

Having the pony so indulged and overfed that it gets colic, and the budgie dies of thirst and neglect.

Raising kids fit enough to play sport dangerously enough to be always incapacitated.

Sleepless nights nursing a sick child who always miraculously recovers in time for that important date.

Being a pedestrian because there are only two cars but three driving licences under the same roof.

Staying home for your kids and having them all go out.

Taking a bath the only time the phone is for you.

Someone taking up bongo drums when everyone else is cramming for exams.

Higher education being so children can appreciate the simplicity and poverty of back-to-nature movements.

Cooking huge dinners that nobody comes home to, or catering for six extra appetites without warning.

Moving into a larger home for the kids, who immediately leave home to crowd in two-bedroom community houses with at least ten of their best friends.

Having a family around is…

…soggy towels, muddy floors, empty larders, noise, chaos.

And contentment.

Acknowledgements

Versions of these stories were previously published as follows:
'The Collecting Instinct' – *Positive Words*, 2011
'The Lost Club' – *Positive Word*s
'Hero's Never Kiss Girls' – *Positive Words,* 2014
'Five Minutes in the Life of…' – *Reaping a Harcest*, Longman Cheshire anthology, 1988; and Australian Broadcasting Commission, Brisbane, *Words and Music* program, 1980
'Pocket Money' – *The Sunday Mail*, Brisbane, 1978; and *Positive Words*, December, 2011
'The Class Raffle', 'A Money Problem' 'School Lunches', 'The School Dance', 'The Delicate Problem', 'Low Finance', 'The Viking Funeral', 'The Lost Football', 'Lost and Found', 'Harmony' – *There Are No Answers,* Ronda Fienberg (1999), Occasional Office, Ringwood, Victoria
'Home Nursing' – *Calling All Houssewives* (VHA), 1975; and *Positive Words*, April 2005
'Crackers' and 'The Good Samaritan'– *Positive Words*, 2014
'School Lunches' – *Family Circle* February 2004; and *Positive Words*, 2012
'The Cooking Disaster' – *Positive Words,* November 2011
'Relationships' – *Positive Words,* November 2009
'How to Diet' *Positive Words,* October 2014
'The Jeans Problem' – *Positive Words*, 2014
'Homework For Parents' – *Woman's Day*, 1973, as 'Homework and Exams'
'The Guinea Pig Business' – Woman's World, 1972, as 'A Matter of Multiplication'
'What to Wear' – *The Sunday Mail*, Brisbane, 1978
'Clean Socks For School' – *Positive Words*, August 2003

'The Good Samaritan' – *Waterline News*, November 2016

'Yoda' – *Unborn Beauty*, ed. Rochelle Manners, Wombat Books, 2008

'Sherry' – *Horses Down Under* (Victoria horse magazine), 2004; and emagazine *alfiedog.com* December 2012

'Having a family…' – Coastlines, *The Centre Coast Courier*'s literary section, 1986

www.ingramcontent.com/pod-product-compliance
Lightning Source LLC
Chambersburg PA
CBHW070919080526
44589CB00013B/1364